Summer

*For Joyce
and the family I didn't know I had,
with love*

Summer

Liturgical resources for May, June and July
including Eastertide and Pentecost

Ruth Burgess

wild goose
publications   www.ionabooks.com

Contents of book © individual contributors
Compilation © 2020 Ruth Burgess

First published 2020 by
Wild Goose Publications, 21 Carlton Court, Glasgow G5 9JP, UK,
the publishing division of the Iona Community.
Scottish Charity No. SC003794. Limited Company Reg. No. SC096243.

ISBN 978-1-84952-724-8

Cover photograph © Zichrini from Pixabay
Internal photograph © Taiftin | Dreamstime.com

The publishers gratefully acknowledge the support of the Drummond Trust,
3 Pitt Terrace, Stirling FK8 2EY in producing this book.

All rights reserved. Apart from the circumstances described below relating to non-commercial use, no part of this publication may be reproduced in any form or by any means, including photocopying or any information storage or retrieval system, without written permission from the publisher.

Non-commercial use: The material in this book may be used non-commercially for worship and group work without written permission from the publisher. If photocopies of sections are made, please make full acknowledgement of the source, and report usage to CLA or other copyright organisation.

Commercial use: For any commercial use, a licence must be obtained in advance from the publisher via PLSclear.com

Ruth Burgess has asserted her right in accordance with the Copyright, Designs and Patents Act, 1988, to be identified as the author of this compilation and the individual contributors have asserted their rights to be identified as authors of their contributions.

Overseas distribution
Australia: Willow Connection Pty Ltd, Unit 4A, 3–9 Kenneth Road,
Manly Vale, NSW 2093
New Zealand: Pleroma, Higginson Street, Otane 4170, Central Hawkes Bay

Printed by Bell & Bain, Thornliebank, Glasgow

Contents

Contents in detail   6

Introduction   13

Summer in May   15

Resurrection appearances   23

Easter is …   67

Stories from the Acts of the Apostles   79

Post-Easter lectionary readings   119

Rogationtide   129

Ascension   147

Summer in June   157

Pentecost   171

Trinity   199

Post-Pentecost lectionary readings   219

Father's Day   247

All creatures great and small   255

Summer in July   263

Summer saints   273

Summer holidays   285

Journeys   293

Pilgrimage and retreat   301

Summer blessings   313

Sources   318

About the authors   319

Index of authors   326

Contents in detail

Summer in May

✹	The swifts' return	16
✹	Bluebells at Whiddon	16
✹	So beautiful	17
((○))	We wait for growth	18
✹	Holy hello	19
✹	Late May's glory	19
▯	Laundry day	20
((○))	In sun and shade	21
♪	Praise God for Easter flowers	22

Key to symbols

✝	Prayer
✢	Biblical reflection
⌬	Liturgy
♪	Song
◭	Story
☻	Script
▯	Reflection
✹	Poem
((○))	Responsive prayer
●	Monologue
U	Child-friendly

Resurrection appearances

☻	It was Sunday night late (John 20:19–31)	24
♪	In praise of doubt	28
✢ U	The man with a huge job (John 20:19–31)	29
✢	Emmaus journey	30
●	Life still felt very raw (Luke 24:13–35)	36
◭ U	They didn't know who he was (Luke 24:13–35)	38
☻	You saw him as well	39
✹	Six handfuls of birds	43
●	It was a strange week	44
▯ U	Doubting Thomas?	46
✢ U	Thomas was always late	47
◭	Flesh, blood, bones	48
♪	Late that evening (John 20:19–29)	52
✢	Looking back (John 21:1–14)	54
● U	One, two, three, four (John 21:1–14)	56
▯ U	Anchovy and zebra fish	58
✝	The fisher-folk of this world	59
♪	I'm going fishing	61
▯	Down-under resurrection	62
●	Breakfast on the shore (John 21:15–25)	62
●	All those slippery fish (John 21:15–25)	64
▯	Some doubted (Matthew 28:16–20)	65

Easter is ...

- 🔲U Easter is ... 68
- ((◎)) When flowers bloom (Opening responses for Eastertide) 68
- 🔲 The birds sang (An Easter litany) 70
- ✟ Let us say that again 71
- 🔲 Easter in spite of myself 72
- ✟ From the dark mornings 73
- 🔲 Easter paths 74
- 🔲 Partners and co-workers 76
- 🔲 The hope in our hearts 78

Stories from the Acts of the Apostles

- ● Dear Theophilus (Acts 1:1–14) 80
- 🔲U Ben's stories (Acts 1:1–14) 81
- 🌀 Home visit (Acts 3:1–10) 83
- 🔲 Be healed (Acts 3:1–10) 84
- 🌀 What did you expect? (Based on Acts 3:1–10) 86
- 🌀 U The puzzling book (Acts 8:26–39) 89
- 🐾 The charioteer's bar room tale (Acts 8:26–39) 90
- ● Ananias' prayers (Acts 9:1–19) 92
- ● U Ananias' story (Acts 9:1–19) 94
- ((◎)) Will something happen to us? (Acts 9:1–19) 96
- 🌀 Spot the similarities (Acts 9:36–43) 96
- 🌀 Behind my story (Acts 9:36–43) 98
- 🌀 We can do it! (Acts 13:1–3,14:8–18) 101
- 🐾 Sydney the chocolate Labrador (Acts 13:1–3,14:8–18) 102
- 🌀 Paul and Lydia (Acts 16:9–15) 104
- ✢ Two very different people (Acts 16:9–15) 107
- ● The business woman (Acts 16:11–15) 108
- 🌀 An old wife's tale (Acts 16:16–40) 110
- 🐾U Jeb the jailer (Acts 16:16–40) 113
- 🔲 Who am I with? (Acts 18:1–4) 114
- 🐾U The best teacher? (Acts 18:1–4) 116

Summer

Post-Easter lectionary readings

- ● The widow of Zarephath (1 Kings 17:1–24)   120
- ✢ He's raving mad (John 10:1–10)   122
- ⌂U Shuggie the shepherd (John 10:1–10)   123
- ✢ I've read these verses at funerals (John 14:1–14)   124
- ✢ The house of many rooms (John 14:1–7)   125
- ● A letter home (John 17:1–26)   126

Rogationtide

- ⊞ Rogationtide   130
- ✟ A prayer for Rogation Sabbath   131
- ⊞ I have seen how light falls   132
- ⊞ Earth's wisdom   132
- ⊞ A new season comes   133
- ⊞ Walking the fields   134
- ⌂U An elemental Rogation liturgy   136

Ascension

- ● Goodbye (Acts 1:1–11)   148
- ☻ Gone (Acts 1:1–11)   149
- ⊞ Ascension questions   151
- ♫ Ascension song   152
- ✟ Ascension prayer   153
- ● We see him (A disciple reflects)   153
- ⊞ Ascension of the Cosmic Christ   155

Summer in June

- ✻ Thirteen orchids   158
- ✢ Ever at play in God's presence (Proverbs 8:30–31)   158
- ✻ Words like birds   159
- ⊞ Why this discontent?   160
- ((◉)) Thank you   161
- ⊞ A summer lament   162
- ✻ Feathered friends   163
- ((◉)) In celebration of your creation   163
- ✟ Appreciating the light   164

	At Alresford Creek 165
🎭	Highland morning 166
🎭	Midsummer 167
📜	Summer solstice 168

Pentecost

((O))	Welcome, Holy Spirit 172
●	When the day of Pentecost had come 172
U	Finding the right words 174
	The beautiful noise of God 175
✝	A brand-new day 176
✝	Come, Holy Spirit 177
✝	Big Spirit 178
🎭 U	Mystery gift 180
✝	Wild Spirit of God 182
✝	Dependency 182
	Without a word 183
((O))	Spirit of Life 185
✝	Light me, Lord 186
📜	A Eucharistic prayer for Pentecost 187
	Holy Spirit – the comforter 191
	Holy Spirit – the disturber 192
🎭	Whitsunday service 192
((O))	For your Spirit 193
●	Transformative Spirit 194
	It's not how I would have done it 196

Key to symbols

✝	Prayer
✥	Biblical reflection
📜	Liturgy
♪	Song
🎭	Story
🎭	Script
	Reflection
🎭	Poem
((O))	Responsive prayer
●	Monologue
U	Child-friendly

Trinity

((O))	Opening responses for Trinity Sunday 200
✝	Prayer of approach for Trinity Sunday 200
●	The disciples (Matthew 28:16–20) 201
🎭 U	Saying goodbye (Matthew 28:16–20) 203
🎭	Awesome Trinity 204
✝	Three in One 207
♪	In the world, God's love declaring 208
((O))	Trinity of grace (A responsive prayer of praise) 209
●	Trinity talk 210

Summer

- ⛪ I am Alpha and Omega   212
- ⛪ Season of Trinity   214
- ⛪♫ God Beyond, God Within and God Between   215
- ✝ A blessing for Trinity Sunday   218

Post-Pentecost lectionary readings

- ● When Sarah laughed and danced (Genesis 18:1–5, 21:8–10)   220
- ❦ A king or a queen? (1 Samuel 8:4–11,16–20)   223
- ✢U We really want a king (1 Samuel 8:4–11, 16–20)   226
- ✢ David is chosen to be king (1 Samuel 15:34–16:13)   227
- ❦ Wee Davy (1 Samuel 17:32–49)   228
- ✢ Deep within (Mark 5:25–34)   230
- ✢ Blessed (Matthew 5:1–12)   231
- ❦ U The sparrows' story (Matthew 10:26–30)   232
- ⛪U Spurgie (Matthew 10:26–30)   235
- ● A cup of cold water (Matthew 10:40–42)   238
- 🕊U A special welcome (Matthew 10:40–42)   239
- ● The sower went forth to sow (Matthew 13:1–9,18–23)   240
- ❦ Gardeners and bonfires (Matthew 13:24–30, 36–43)   242
- ❦U Noah's big picnic (John 6:1–14)   244

Father's Day

- ((◉)) Like a father to us   248
- ⛪ Dads and summer   249
- ⛪ Father and son   250
- ((◉)) Let us pray for fathers   252
- ✝ A Father's Day blessing (based on Psalm 121)   253

All creatures great and small

- ♫ The animals in the zoo   256
- 🦋 Little monsters   257
- 🦋 This far north   258
- 🦋 June in the Danube Delta   258
- 🦋 Birdsong   259
- 🦋 The trouble with adders   260

Contents in detail   11

▣   Goats don't do *metanoia*   261
✣   The wasps and the midges   262

Summer in July

☦   For warm seaside days   264
▣   Summer in Skye   264
▣   Summer season   265
✣   The sun is shining   265
♪   The Alpha and the Omega   266
✣   Tiptoe through the tulips   267
((○))   For the sun's rising   268
▣   A summer visit to Flanders   269
((○))   Rainbow God (A prayer for Pride)   270
((○))   For sunlight dancing   271

Key to symbols	
☦	Prayer
✢	Biblical reflection
⌀	Liturgy
♪	Song
▨	Story
☺	Script
▣	Reflection
✣	Poem
((○))	Responsive prayer
●	Monologue
U	Child-friendly

Summer saints

☦   As children to a mother (A prayer for Julian's Day, 13th May)   274
♪   Remembering Julian   274
☦   Eucharistic prayer of thanksgiving for Julian's Day   275
▣   All will be well (A Mother Julian reflection)   276
▣   The monk from Jarrow   278
☦   Aldersgate Sunday   279
☦   A heart strangely warmed (Aldersgate Sunday, 24th May)   279
✣   Heroes   280
♪   Prayer for St Columba's Day   281
♪   Saint Pat and Saint Colum   281
♪   It's hard to enter the kingdom   282
▣   St Swithun was here   283
▣   Holy Fools (For 1st July, the Feast of St Simeon, the Holy Fool)   284

Summer holidays

☦   A teacher's prayers at the end of a school year   286
((○))   God of holidays   288
▣   A very British summer   289
☦   We thank you   290
▣   Two whole months of glorious freedom   290
✣   Down at the harbour   291

Summer

Journeys

- 🌿 Toddling forward   294
- 🔲 U   Journey on the roads in Cameroon   294
- 🔲 The red scooter   296
- 🔲 Mom's feet   297
- 🔲 It's a funny old journey   298
- ✝ Travel with me   299
- ✠ I am still with you   300

Pilgrimage and retreat

- 🔲 I search for you   302
- 🔲 The cove (Remembering a Devon childhood)   304
- ✝ St Queran's Well, Troqueer   305
- ✝ Malta retreat   306
- 🔲 The well   308
- 🔲 Chester Cathedral   309
- 🌿 Back where I started   310
- 🎵 There is a Christ, and he sails the storm   311

Summer blessings

- ✝ An all-day summer blessing   314
- 🎵 Bless all who worship you   314
- ✝ May God our Creator   315
- ✝ The blessing of the God of life   315
- ✝ A joyful summer blessing   316
- ✝ God bless   316
- ✝ May long summer days   317

Key to symbols

✝	Prayer
✠	Biblical reflection
✍	Liturgy
🎵	Song
🍃	Story
🎭	Script
🔲	Reflection
🌿	Poem
(((○)))	Responsive prayer
●	Monologue
U	Child-friendly

Introduction

Summer follows *Spring*.

Summer is a liturgical resource book that covers the months of May, June and July. It includes prayers, responses, stories, poems, liturgies, songs, reflections, scripts and monologues for the Christian seasons of Eastertide and Pentecost, as well as Saints' days, Rogationtide and Ascension. There are also poems for summertime and reflections on pilgrimage, holidays and retreats.

The resources are written by members, associate members and friends of the Iona Community and others.

I've defined the season by the month that contains the solstice or equinox and the month either side of it.

As the date of Easter changes each year, I have chosen to include material for Lent and Easter morning in *Spring*, the previous volume of this series, and material for Easter evening and Eastertide in this volume, *Summer*.

Thank you to all the contributors for their rich and imaginative material that I have been privileged to edit.

Given the quality and amount of material that was contributed to this book and its predecessors, *Winter* and *Spring*, completing the series in due course with *Autumn* promises to be a surprise and a delight.

Thank you, too, to the Wild Goose Publications team, particularly to Sandra Kramer and Neil Paynter, whose advice, wisdom, cheery e-mails and attention to detail over the years I have valued greatly.

This year, with many countries in lockdown due to the presence of COVID-19, we look forward – with great hope – to the return of summer.

Raspberries

All the year round
I can buy them pre-packed
on the supermarket shelves,
and sometimes I do.

But to fiercely prune them
talk to them
stake them
water them
watch the bees buzz around them
feel the sun warming them
protect them from interested birds
nurture them
see their colour deepen
watch them swell to ripeness
smell their promise of sweetness

and then to pick them
their juice staining my fingers
and to eat them …

Wow!
Ripe raspberries.

It's summertime.

Rejoice!

– Ruth Burgess

Summer in May

The swifts' return

Each year, we wait to hear their coming:
screeching to skim our tiles,
swooping to sip the air's deliciousness
in scrolls, curved and carved
from marbled clouds.
They follow unseen streets, straight
as sunrays, riding the winds' miles,
sleeping on crescent wings, defying
desert, forest, ocean,
beach and cliff. Now here.
Finding again the small welcome
of our roofs, hobbling
on knuckled feet, to lay their eggs.

Each year we wait. And wonder.
Marvel at their return to us
in scimitars of light,
their soaring ecstasy,
their young, tumbling to instant flight.
Each year we search the skies,
our ears tuned to different frequencies
to be the first to hear their circling screams,
or see them hurling down to us. To be
the first to say: the swifts have come again.

Janet Killeen

Bluebells at Whiddon

How do you begin to describe the ishness of bluebells?
They cascade down the hillside rushing over rocks
through shade and sun, glide round trees in sinuous curves,
with beech and oak leaves, newborn, providing their canopy.
Are they shoals gathered together for safety?
You may pick off one or two or even more,
but the shoal is safe to reproduce for another year.

Their blue out-blues the sky that looks pallid in comparison.
I drink in the blue, one draught after another, knowing that
the bells have but a short life. Gorse and broom sprout yellow
and they are beautiful too but it is that deep blue
that somehow seeps inside my eyes and slakes my thirst –
a seasonal wine that leaves me dizzy and lost for words.

John Randall

So beautiful

So beautiful.
Cherry blossom descending silent as snow.
Nature's confetti,
pink mantle for the grass.
Enjoy its twirling downward dance.
This too must pass.

Hawthorn blossom cascades.
Bridal bouquets,
pure, virginal, abundant,
grace a myriad of bushes
full of joy, energy of life,
promising a pregnancy of red berries
in due time.

Garden wild with colour.
Tissue-paper thin, the poppies sway,
red dancing loveliness.
Roses peach, yellow, white, crimson
stand solid, steady,
buds ready to burst
into volcanic eruptions of colour.
Pansies peep from pots
and the daisies stretch upwards
worshipping the sun.

Mary Hanrahan

We wait for growth

As the elements give life,
soil and air, sun and rain
providing nurture,
We wait for growth;
we hope for new life.

With restless impatience
that counts the minutes,
wanting it *now*,
We wait for growth;
we hope for new life.

With steady patience,
trusting roots buried
deep in the ground,
We wait for growth;
we hope for new life.

With ceaseless work,
the strenuous effort
of trying to make a difference,
We wait for growth;
we hope for new life.

With unforced hope,
living in anticipation
of days yet to come,
We wait for growth;
we hope for new life.

In effort and expectation,
in work and rest,
in doing and being,
We wait for growth;
we hope for new life.

Jan Berry

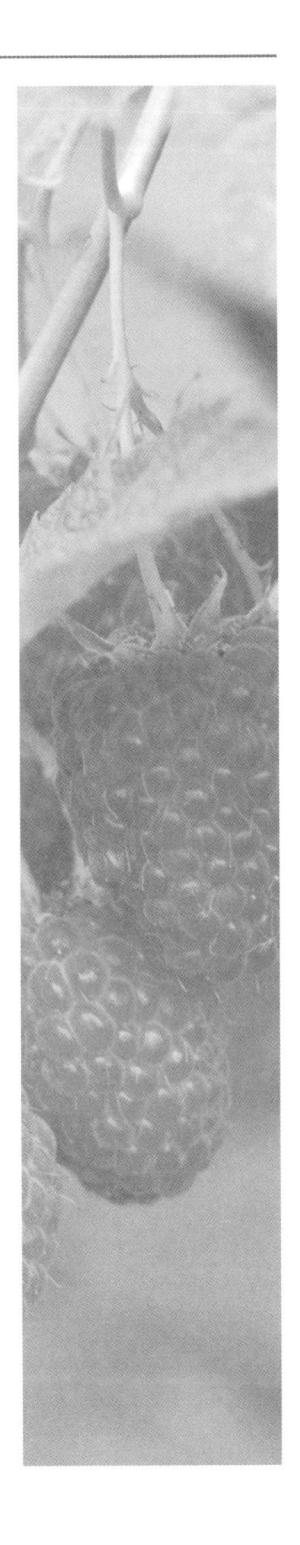

Holy hello

I plant the plant.
Intone a chant:
'Grow, grow, grow'
then let it be.

It's not for me
to know how it will go.
I have no power
to make buds flower.

But I say even though
the seeds are sown,
what is grown
is God's love saying 'Hello'.

Stuart Barrie

Late May's glory

Hawthorn hedges run amok,
dresses trailing whiter
than any wedding frock,
announcing summer.
Leaves of beech and oak
willing the late uncurling ash
to join the canopy
where young birds sing rejoicingly.

Seven weeks of Easter,
we should be ready now
as nature is
for whatever summer
and the Holy Spirit bring.

Liz Gregory-Smith

Laundry day

I am an ordinary woman
hanging out the washing
in a warm summer breeze.
However, like Jesus' mother,
I ponder in my heart,
today on the inevitable
imperfection of human love
which seems always to be
wounded and wounding.
Without evil intention
we harm and are harmed,
seeking in the other
what the other cannot give.
However many lights
one turns on in hope,
shrewd observers know
if nobody is in residence.
In arbitrary movement
of benevolent wind,
I use the last clothes peg,
pick up the empty basket,
head back to the house,
the commonplace locus
of my incompetent love.

Bonnie Thurston

In sun and shade

Glory be to God in the world around us:
in sun and shade, day and night,
and the rhythms of the seasons.
Glory be to God!

Glory be to God in the community in which we live:
in love and laughter, sorrow and joy,
and the patterns of human living.
Glory be to God!

Glory be to God in the way we live our lives:
in giving and sharing, thanking and knowing,
and all that makes us Jesus' disciples.
Glory be to God!

Glory be to God in the world:
in the search for justice and peace,
and all that makes us one human family.
Glory be to God!

Glory be to God in the smallest of things:
in tiny creatures, fleeting moments,
the smallest seed of faith new-growing.
Glory be to God!

Glory be to God in greatness and majesty:
in the tallest mountains, the highest clouds,
the awesome dance of the whole cosmos.
Glory be to God!

Glory be to you, O God,
Father, Son and Holy Spirit,
now and for ever. **Amen**

Richard Sharples

Praise God for Easter flowers

(Tune: 'Rhosymedre')

Praise God for Easter flowers
that cover all the earth,
their vibrant glowing colours,
a promise of new birth.
Praise God for all his love and care:
His glory displayed everywhere,
His glory displayed everywhere.

Praise God for morning dew
that sparkles all around,
with myriad shimmering hues
refreshing thirsty ground.
Praise God for all his love and care:
His glory displayed everywhere,
His glory displayed everywhere.

Praise God for risen life
with each and every breath;
and praise the living Christ
who conquers fear and death.
Praise God for all his love and care:
His glory displayed everywhere,
His glory displayed everywhere.

Carol Dixon

Resurrection appearances

It was Sunday night late

(John 20:19–31)

(You can use some or all of these stories.)

Disciples (7 voices):

A: It was Sunday night late
   and we were all together.
   John and Peter had told us
   what they'd seen at the tomb,
   and Mary had told us
   that she had met Jesus in the garden.

B: It was Sunday night late
   and we were talking and talking,
   and we had the doors locked
   because we were afraid
   of the Jewish authorities.

C: It was Sunday night late
   and Jesus came,
   and he stood in the middle of the room,
   and he said: 'Peace be with you.'
   And we didn't know what to do or say.

D: It was Sunday night late
   and Jesus showed us his hands
   and the scar on his side,
   and we began to believe
   and we whooped with joy!

E: It was Sunday night late
   and he said it again.
   'Peace be with you.'
   And he breathed on us –
   he brought us to life
   and we were full of God's Spirit.

F: It was Sunday night late
and he told us:
'As God sent me,
so I am sending you.
The Holy Spirit is in you.'

G: It was Sunday night late
and the doors were locked,
and we were all together
and Jesus was with us.

What a night!

Thomas:

I missed him.
I missed seeing Jesus.
I wasn't with the others when he came.

They seem so sure.
They told me what he'd said.
They'd seen the scars on his body.
They said he'd breathed on them
and they felt strong and sure and awake and alive.

And I told them,
I told them straight:
'Unless I see him too,
unless I can see his scars and touch them,
I can't believe.'

Jesus came back a week later
and I was there.
And he looked round the room
and he wished us peace.

Peace, I needed that.
And he came over to me

and invited me to touch his scars,
and he told me to stop doubting,
to believe that it was really him
and he was alive.

I looked at him
and the words came out of me,
I don't know where they came from.
I told him: 'You are my Lord and my God.'

That's my story.
I missed him
and he came back and found me.
He knew what I was like,
he knew what I'd said
and he wanted me to see him and believe.

Jesus:

Thomas.
Ah, Thomas.
Thomas the twin.
Thomas, one of the twelve.
Thomas, my disciple.

You know, Thomas,
they'll always remember you
when they come to tell
the stories of my resurrection.

They'll find a name for you, you know;
they'll call you Doubting Thomas,
that's how you'll be remembered.

Don't look at me like that, Thomas.
I know there's more to you than doubting.
You ask good questions, Thomas,
you help others to know what's going on.

I love you, Thomas.
I'll always love you.
You belong in my story.

And you know,
because of you, Thomas,
a lot of other questioners
will know that I love them too.

The scribe:

Me, I'm the scribe.
I'm trying to write down the stories
that people are telling me about Jesus –
and it's some job I tell you!

You know what I've noticed?
He wasn't afraid to say what he thought.
And he talked to everybody:
religious people,
soldiers,
women on the streets,
children,
everybody.

And he did such extraordinary things.
He silenced a storm.
He brought a child back to life.
He turned water into wine.
He walked through closed doors
and he healed people.

And he told stories,
wonderful stories:
stories about feasts and builders
and tiny seeds,
about kings
and judges
and buried treasure.

And I'm trying to write it all down
and I know I won't manage it.
There's too many stories to fit into one book
but I hope you enjoy reading what I've recorded.

May what I've written bring you love and life.
May this book help you to love God
and to walk with Jesus.

Ruth Burgess, Spill the Beans

In praise of doubt

(Tune: 'Forest green')

Some people say, to doubt is wrong.
We should not doubt at all.
To question our beliefs, they say,
could bring about our fall.
But doubt permits an honest stance
in those who are devout.
For those who think about beliefs
can sing in praise of doubt.

The Thomas story has been used
to judge, condemn, deplore;
but Thomas shows he is sincere.
He wanted to be sure.
For doubt can help but not deter
a vital turnabout.
Yes! Those who care about beliefs
can sing in praise of doubt.

If our beliefs prevent our search
for new and different creeds,
let us beware of narrow views
where dogma often breeds.

With new, exciting facts we learn
much love can come about.
Yes! Those who grow in their beliefs
can sing in praise of doubt.

George Stuart

The man with a huge job
(John 20:19–31)

In the Bible reading today there's a message from the person who wrote the book we call John's Gospel. He was probably called John, but we don't know his family name.

He had a huge job. He asked people who knew Jesus to tell him what they could remember about what Jesus did and said. And then he tried to write it all down and make it into a book.

There were hundreds of stories. Someone remembered how Jesus had healed people. Someone remembered a story about Jesus at a wedding. Some people remembered how Jesus had died. One of the disciples told him how Jesus had come to meet them when they were fishing.

John had a problem. There were so many stories that they would not fit into one book. So he did what all people writing books have to do. He had to choose which stories to put in. And he did.

When John had nearly finished his book he thought that it would be a good idea to tell people what he had done. So he wrote down a sentence in his book that said that Jesus had done so many things – that he couldn't fit them all into his book. But he hoped that the stories he had written down would help his readers to know how much Jesus cared about people and loved them.

I sometimes wonder about the stories that John had to leave out – but it was so long ago that we'll never be able to find out what they were.

Can you remember some of the stories about Jesus that you've been told?

If you were making a book about Jesus and you could choose three stories to put in – which ones would you choose?

If there's time, you could make a small book now of your own favourite stories.

Ruth Burgess, Spill the Beans

Emmaus journey

There's that moment, that split second after you wake up, when everything feels normal. Then it hits you and it feels like you've been trampled to the ground all over again.

That's what grief does to you.

Yes, it's different for everybody. But for me, it was the numbness. That sense that I wasn't quite living in the same world; an unreality, probably a self-protection from the worst of the pain. It lasts and lasts, that phase. Even though it looked like I was going through the motions, functioning, inside the same questions were on repeat. Nothing really mattered apart from those. It was hell.

The worst thing was not being able to get those images out of my mind. I didn't want to see him suffer – but I couldn't leave him either. Not that I followed him that closely – I'm ashamed to say I was too cowardly for that. I didn't run as far as the other disciples – didn't abandon him to that extent – but they had more to lose than I did. They were the inner circle, his closest companions. I would hardly have been recognised; it was more dangerous for them. But still, I only saw from a distance; from the back of the crowd. Not like the women – I don't know how they did it; how they could stand to be at the foot of the cross; how they could look on the cruelty, the blood, the pain.

He'd done nothing to deserve it. To me, he was the most godly person I'd ever met. When we were on the road, he'd always be the first up. He'd be up a hill somewhere, or in a garden, praying. He'd come back to us with his face shining, hungry for his breakfast, eager to lead us on to some new village, or to speak to a crowd. He always looked out for the people no one else bothered with. That's why we were all there – there were even tax-collectors among us! People's background was no issue to him – it was what he saw in them that mattered. He looked for that spark of faith, that willingness to see beyond what they taught in the Temple and to catch a glimpse of God instead.

He looked for humility – but everyone knew that we didn't all have that! When he was out meeting people he made special time for those who didn't usually get a look in. He'd talk to women, those with defiling diseases – he'd touch lepers! He was delighted to speak to children. He mingled with Gentiles and people with anti-social behaviour. He was all for the folk the system left behind.

You should have heard him talk! The stories he wove! He had everyone dangling on a thread, completely rapt, and even when he'd finished you'd be thinking about what he'd said for days. It was never quite as straightforward as you thought, not when he got started on those parables.

We had a blast. Sleeping on boats, walking from village to village, relying on hospitality, sometimes feasting, sometimes eating the grain from the fields. Sometimes our bellies were empty; sometimes we were invited to the best places in town, enjoying the hospitality of Pharisees even; and there was always Mary and Martha's place.

It was a good life – until he started talking about his suffering. None of us wanted to hear that. We always thought one day he'd probably do something decisive, try to take on the Romans – but not suffering … not that. I was troubled by his talk of taking up the cross. It sent shivers through us all – we knew what those Romans were like, we'd seen the crosses, knew how finely they'd tuned those instruments of torture. 'No, Jesus – don't talk about crosses.'

But once he'd started he couldn't stop. It was as though he knew – even last week when we shared the Passover, he talked about his body being broken, as he tore the bread; he poured out wine, and talked about his blood being spilled and a new covenant sealed. He said one of us would betray him. Turned out we all did.

After that it was all a blur. Everything happened so quickly. We were asleep in the garden and we woke to the sounds of an angry crowd. They arrested him, and most of us ran. I'm ashamed now. But after he was crucified – I can hardly say it – after he was crucified, I just wanted to sleep for a thousand years.

It was Cleopas who persuaded me it was time to go home – to go back home to Emmaus; to put it all behind us. Jesus had failed. All his words had come to nothing. He was no use dead. We had wanted so much for him to be the one to change things. We thought, with his determination and compassion, with his fresh way of looking at things, he might just be the one we'd all been waiting for.

When we heard the terrible lies being spread about him, we knew we had to get out of Jerusalem. Those women should never have followed him to the cross. It turned their minds. They started saying that he wasn't dead at all – that they'd visited the tomb and found angels there, who told them that he was alive. I felt sorry for them but there was nothing I could do. So with Cleopas I headed for home.

It was the longest journey of my life. You see, for all the trouble of the last week, for all the disappointment and the loss, I did love him. You couldn't not. There was just something about him. He was wide open somehow – he had a depth and wisdom I'd never encountered before. It was as though he could see right into your soul. But you didn't mind because he made you feel safe and loved. You could be vulnerable with him – and you could tell he liked you; that he enjoyed being with you. He made you feel special. I know it wasn't just me who felt like that – it was everyone. Everyone who met him went away feeling better – apart from the rich young man who had everything, and Jesus told him to get rid of all his wealth – that was a good one! As if he'd do that! Oh, and Nicodemus, who just got confused (but I think he came good in the end). And he upset a few religious people, especially when he started throwing tables around in the Temple. He was only angry because they were excluding the people who needed God most. Anyway, I knew that as long as I lived there'd never be anyone else like Jesus. So I was grieving for him, grieving as I turned my back on Jerusalem; I was grieving and numb. I knew I needed to put all that Jesus stuff behind me and just move on with my life. I didn't want to – but I didn't have a choice. It was all over. I'd have to start all over again – and maybe one day it wouldn't seem quite so painful, living without Jesus.

As we put one heavy foot in front of the other, Cleopas and I talked about all these things.

We weren't the only ones leaving Jerusalem that day. We weren't far into the journey when a stranger joined us. He wanted to know what we were talking about. There was only one thing to talk about! Hadn't he been in Jerusalem? Didn't he know? How can he not have heard that Jesus was dead? Didn't he see Jesus riding into Jerusalem on the donkey that day? Hadn't he seen the crowds? Didn't he know about the scandal of the famous preacher finally meeting his end at Passover time? Hadn't he smelt the blood and the fear, and seen the sky go so dark?

The funny thing was, as much as we had to tell him, he had more to tell us. For someone who didn't know about the crucifixion of Jesus, he seemed to have a lot of theories about it! He reckoned that Jesus was the one the prophets had talked about; the one longed for since the days of Moses. He knew his scriptures inside out! He seemed to think that the suffering was all part of the plan. I couldn't see it myself, but what our companion was saying was mesmerising! Somehow my heart and my legs didn't seem so heavy when he was speaking – so I was amazed when we reached our door. I'd hardly noticed that darkness had fallen.

He made to go on further, but we called him back. We couldn't let him wander into the dark, dangerous night. Terrible things happened in darkness. Anyway, we wanted to hear more of what he had to say. So we invited him in.

We prepared a simple supper for him to share with us, and we sat at the table.

You won't believe this, but something happened when he picked up the bread. He lifted it up, said a blessing, and broke it, and as he gave it to us, we saw it was Jesus! We were just about to speak his name and he vanished! He just disappeared from our sight.

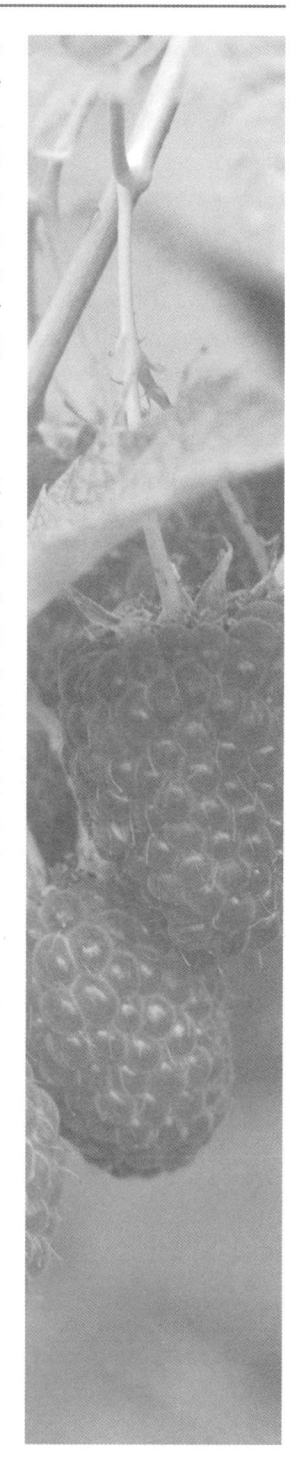

Cleopas and I clutched each other. It was him! It was really him! We couldn't believe it but we'd both seen it. As the shock wore off, we realised that those women had been right! Somehow, Jesus was not dead. He was not dead at all. We hadn't imagined it – he'd been with us! He'd talked to us and made our hearts burn. He was real.

Immediately we knew what we had to do. We had to get back to Jerusalem – to tell the other disciples what we'd seen. We had to tell them that Jesus was alive! And we had to go back to see what Jesus wanted of us – how we could still be his followers. We realised that maybe it hadn't all ended after all!

Suddenly the dark dangerous night didn't matter any more. We grabbed our cloaks, slammed the door behind us and sped all the way back to Jerusalem – in record time! This time there were wings on our feet, not rocks in our socks!

The disciples were where we left them. When we burst into the room, they were already animated and excited. We weren't the only ones to have seen Jesus. He'd appeared to Peter. We told them that we'd seen him too – that we'd recognised him when he broke bread.

We stayed there, laughing and celebrating – waiting to see what would happen next.

And do you know – he actually came back! He came and stood among us, and said 'Peace be with you'. He ate some fish and told us he'd got a job for us to do – that we were to proclaim forgiveness and be his witnesses; to tell the good news that nothing could defeat God's love in Jesus. He promised his power to help us.

After that the stories just kept coming in! Night after night there was news of fresh encounters. He'd appeared to Thomas and had offered up his scarred hands; he had awaited the disciples on a beach, cooking breakfast, and called Peter to care for his people. Peter was so emotional that night – he'd thought there would never be a way back after what he'd done. Jesus had made it right again.

Everywhere Jesus went he turned things round. Where there was sadness, he brought joy and hope. He didn't seem to mind that everyone he met had let him down! Our shame was swallowed by the overwhelming joy of being in his presence and knowing that love had had the last word.

I think it's always going to be the same. You never know when you are going to encounter him next. You'll just be aware that he's there – you'll feel a warmth and a gentleness and a peace. It will probably be when you least expect it. It will probably be when you're worn down with sadness or numb with grief; he'll squeeze in beside you and hold your hand. Sometimes he'll wear the disguise of a friend or stranger, in the right place at the right time, lending you strength and comfort.

I have to be honest with you, there are times, still, when he feels far away. It might be the same for you – phases of doubt and emptiness. Jesus knew those times too. When he was on the cross, the women heard him say that God had abandoned him. He must have felt absolutely desolate to be reciting Psalm 22, which begins 'My God, my God, why have you abandoned me?' But Jesus will have known the end of the Psalm: 'He did not despise or abhor the affliction of the afflicted; he did not hide his face from me, but heard when I cried to him.' On that cross, Jesus knew that God was still with him – that God was hanging, pierced with nails and suffering – and that God joined in with his cries. You see – Jesus will always hear you. Even when you can't feel it, he's still with you. That's when he's with you the most.

And so you will meet Jesus many times on your journey through life. You'll know him in unexpected generosity, unreserved kindness. You'll know him in the most ordinary gestures – but something in them will open your heart, and you will know it's him. Most of all, you will know that nothing – not even the cross – can separate you from his Love.

Louise Gough

Life still felt very raw
(Luke 24:13–35)

I wasn't sure what to do next –
life still felt very raw and different.
The angels at the tomb had done their best,
but dressing up in dazzling clothes was not a good idea!
The women were terrified,
and to make it worse
Peter and the others did not believe them.
And although Peter saw the empty tomb for himself
he still has no idea what has happened to me.

I decided in the end to walk alongside two of my friends
who were returning to Jerusalem that evening.
If I listened in to their conversation
it might give me a clue as to what they were thinking.

So that's what I did.
They didn't recognise me
and I was able to ask them what they'd been talking about.

As I'd guessed,
they were talking about what had happened to me in Jerusalem.
They looked so sad.
Cleopas assumed that I was a stranger to Jerusalem
and he told me all about the events of the last few days.
He told me how they'd hoped that I was the Messiah,
the One who would set Israel free.
And then he told me how the women had talked about angels
and a message that I was still alive
and how they had gone to the tomb and found it empty –
and there was no sign of any angels or me!

How little they seemed to have understood what I had taught them!
I couldn't help myself.
I launched into a major lecture on the scriptures,
referencing all the teachings about the Messiah.
I began with Moses and continued through the prophets –
a seven-mile Bible study!

I was on a roll!
I meant to leave them when they reached the village.
I had other people to see
and I had plenty to think about,
but they were hospitable people
and they urged me to eat with them
and to stay with them for the night.
It was almost evening.

So I stayed.
And as we sat at the table
I took the bread, blessed it and broke it
as I had done so often before when we had shared a meal –
and immediately I was no longer a stranger to them.
They recognised me.
And I knew that it was time to go.

From what they said afterwards it was obvious
that my interpretation of the scriptures had struck home.
They had begun to grasp the truth that I was alive again,
but it took the familiar actions and prayers at the meal table
for them to know who I was.

And bless them,
they were desperate to tell the others,
and they got up from the table
and walked the whole seven long miles back to Jerusalem.

And when they found the others
they discovered that, while they had been walking,
I had managed to speak to Simon.

It had been a long day
for me
and for them,
the first day of new life.

This risen life was going to take some getting used to.

Ruth Burgess, Spill the Beans

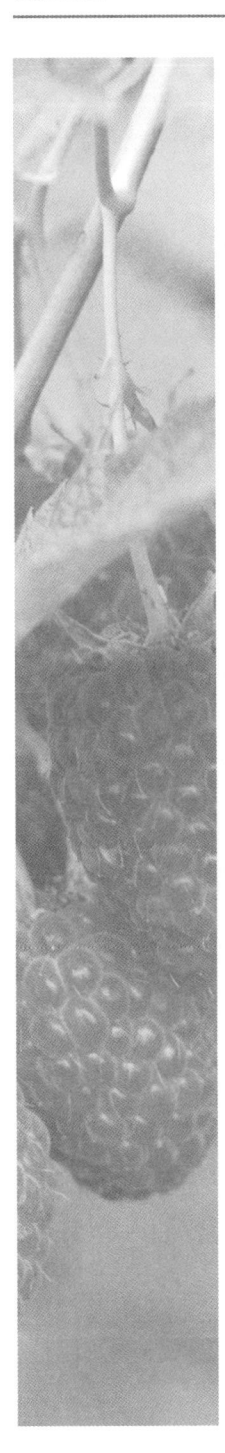

They didn't know who he was

(Luke 24:13–35)

There was a sound in the village that everyone knew, and the children looked forward to it. On Wednesday nights at about 5 o'clock, there was a tune played, a special tune – it was the tune of the ice-cream van. And everyone knew that if they went to the village green, just beside the postbox, there would be a pink-and-green van, and the man who drove it would be in the back of the van ready to sell them an ice cream. John and Alison were usually first in the queue.

Sometimes when they had gone into town the children heard the sound of a siren and they tried to guess which kind of vehicle would come round the corner. It might be a police car with flashing blue lights, or an ambulance or a huge red fire-engine.

One day at school John had been watching his teacher, and he had noticed his teacher tapping his fingers on the desk. He told Alison about it. He said, 'I think our teacher taps his fingers on the table when he's waiting for someone to put their hand up.' Alison laughed. 'My teacher does that too,' she said, 'and sometimes she taps her feet as well.'

The next day Alison and John were talking to their friends Raj and Surrinder; they were talking about members of their families. John and Alison's granny had a special way of doing a jigsaw: she always found all the edge pieces first and joined them together. Raj and Surrinder's uncle had a bell on his bicycle. If they heard it ringing, they knew that their uncle was coming round the corner.

John and Alison's grandad had once been in a pantomime. At first they hadn't recognised him, but when he began to speak they had recognised his voice.

Surrinder told them that once, when she was small, their big brother had dressed up and her mum and dad had told her that he was a visitor who had come to tea. Surrinder had been very polite to the visitor. When the visitor was asked if he'd like sugar in his tea, he put five spoonfuls in and then stirred his tea very very slowly. And Surrinder had guessed who he was. Only her big brother had five spoonfuls of sugar in his tea and stirred the sugar in very very slowly.

There's a story in the Bible about Jesus walking from Jerusalem to Emmaus with two of his friends. He talked with them but they didn't recognise him. They didn't know who he was. When they reached Emmaus his friends invited him in to supper. Jesus did what he always did at mealtimes: he broke the bread into pieces and he said a prayer of thanks to God. And when he did that his friends knew who he was.

Ruth Burgess, Spill the Beans

You saw him as well

A and B: Disciples from the road to Emmaus
C and D: Disciples in Upper Room
E and F: Women followers of Jesus
Mary: Mary Magdalene
John
Peter

All the characters apart from A and B are present at the start. A and B enter and speak.

A: He's alive!

B: We've seen him!

A: He met us on the road home to Emmaus and talked to us about the Messiah.

B: Quoted from the scriptures.

A: But still we didn't recognise him!

B: Then, when we got to the village, we invited him in for supper, and when he broke the bread – then we knew.

A: He vanished – and we had to come to tell you – but it really was him. He's alive!

C: But he was here – in this room. It must have been about the same time as he was walking with you!

D: He came in through the locked door. What did he say?

All: 'Peace be with you!'

C: He showed us the wounds in his hands and side.

D: Invited us to touch him, so we knew it really was him.

C: But we would have known him anyway – known him anywhere!

D: He even asked us for something to eat.

C: We gave him some fish we had left over!

Mary: But when I saw him, he told me not to touch him!

B: You saw him as well?!

D: The women saw him first – they met him near the tomb.

F: We were all there, both Marys, Joanna, Salome and the rest of us.

E: We got up early this morning to go to the tomb to anoint his body.

F: There hadn't been time before the Sabbath began.

E: And we were wondering how to move the stone.

F: Wondering if the soldiers would be there, if they would help us!

E: But when we got there, the tomb was open – the stone rolled to the side.

F: And the body was missing, although the grave clothes were there.

E: We didn't know what to do.

F: And then two men appeared.

E: They were angels!

F: We were frightened.

E: They told us not to look for the living among the dead.

F: And reminded us that Jesus had said he would rise on the third day after he was crucified.

C: Why did we forget that?

E: So we rushed off to tell the rest of you.

F: And then, there he was, in front of us, and we knelt before him and clasped his feet – it was incredible!

E: But Mary Magdalene stayed behind.

Mary: I couldn't leave the garden; it was my only contact with him. It was such a beautiful morning, the sun shining and the grass wet with dew, but tears were streaming down my face and I could hardly see anything properly, so when I saw a man in the garden I thought it must be the gardener, and so asked him what he had done with Jesus' body!

He just said 'Mary', and I knew it was him, no one else said my name quite like that – I wanted to hug him, never let him go again, but he told me not to. He said he hadn't been to the Father yet; but he told me to go and tell you all that he was alive, and I did, but when I got here – you all knew. The other women had seen him as well and had told you!

F: But they didn't believe us at first.

E: 'Silly hysterical women!' they said.

F: But John and Peter *did* rush off to see for themselves.

John: We needed to find out exactly what had happened. I got there first, but hesitated to go into the tomb, but Peter, as usual, rushed straight in.

Peter: And it was just as the women had said: an empty tomb, but the grave clothes left.

John: Then the angels appeared to us!

Peter: And told us in no uncertain terms that we really should have known all this would happen.

John: Jesus had tried to tell us often enough!

C: So what do we do now?

D: Did someone say something about going back to Galilee?

C: Perhaps we should wait a bit and see if he comes again.

A: But anyway, what really matters is that we've all seen him and we know that he's alive!

D: Well – not quite all. Does anyone know where Thomas is?

Helen Barrett

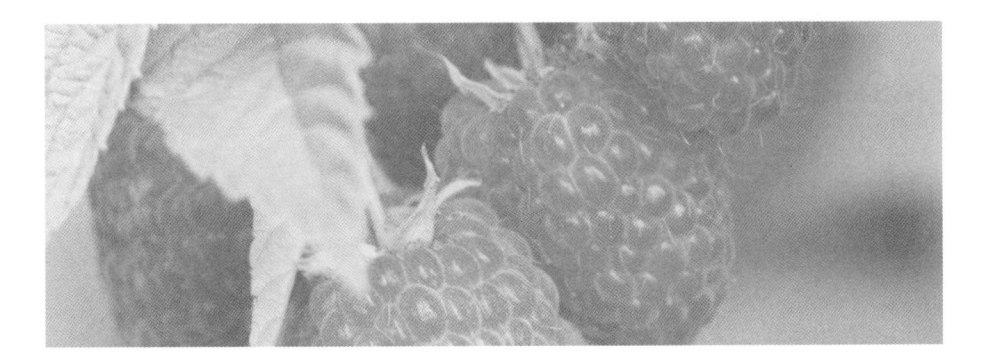

Six handfuls of birds

'Aimer purement, c'est consentir à la distance …'
('To love purely, is to consent to distance …')
Simone Weil

On a train to Edinburgh
I relieve the tedium of a routine journey
by counting on my fingers
each time I see a bird or birds in flight.
So by the time we reach Falkirk
my hands have been filled with birds many times over.
Six times, to be precise: six handfuls of birds.

They are, of course, out of my reach; way above my head,
their purposes inscrutable, their destinations unknown,
their lives forever closed to me, as mine is to them.
But could I have grasped them, closed my hand over them,
they would have been dead things, robbed of their intentions,
not my distant fellow-travellers
journeying together with me
for a brief moment.

Is this what loving is,
this attentive waiting, this looked-for surprise,
this awareness of the distance of a companion on the road,
this sense of fullness on ungrasping hands?

And is this too what it is like
being loved into existence – the hands filled with you
opening, leaving you to be
in your element?

James Munro

It was a strange week

It was a strange week.
I really felt for Thomas.
The rest of us had seen Jesus and he hadn't.

Mary had told us all that Jesus had spoken to her,
early in the morning, in the garden
but we weren't sure whether to believe her or not.

Then, in the evening, we had been together in the house,
except for Thomas.
I don't know why he wasn't there.
And suddenly Jesus was there with us.
He showed his hands, where the nails had cut into them,
and his side where the soldier had pierced him.
And he spoke to us,
about wrongdoing and forgiveness,
and when he came close to each of us
we felt his warm breath.

Jesus was warm and alive. We knew it. He was full of life.

All week we talked about it.
Peter and John told again and again of their visit to the empty tomb.
Mary reminded us of what Jesus had said to her in the garden.
We talked about the marks in his hands and side.
We remembered what he said to us about the Holy Spirit.

All week we talked
and Thomas listened.
And he said to us
that unless he saw Jesus for himself
he would not believe that Jesus was alive.

We wondered if Jesus would come to the house again.
We had heard of other people meeting him,
walking along the road.

And then,
as the week turned,
Jesus came to the house again
and he sought out Thomas.
And Jesus showed Thomas the marks of the nails and the spear
and Thomas, like us,
knew that Jesus was alive.

Jesus said something strange to us after he'd talked with Thomas.
He told us that we were happy and blessed because we'd seen him.
And we were.
Then he said that some people would believe who he was,
and that he was alive, without seeing him,
and they would be happy and blessed too.
I don't get it.
How can people believe in him
when they haven't seen him
or heard his stories
or walked with him along the street.

How will they know who Jesus is?

Ruth Burgess, Spill the Beans

Doubting Thomas?

Have your friends ever talked about something that happened to them when you weren't there?

Maybe they'd seen a film that was on at the cinema when you were visiting your granny?

Maybe you'd been sick when there was something exciting happening at school?

Maybe you missed watching a match where your favourite team won?

Although people tell you about things you've missed, it's not quite the same as being there, is it?

There's a story in the Bible about a man called Thomas who missed seeing Jesus.

Most of Jesus' friends were in a room together on the first Easter Sunday evening.

Jesus came to them and talked with them and showed them that he really was alive. But Thomas wasn't there.

And however much everyone told Thomas that Jesus was alive, Thomas didn't believe them. He told them that unless he saw Jesus for himself, he couldn't believe that Jesus had come back to life.

It was a long week before Jesus came back to see his friends, and this time Thomas was with them. And Jesus talked with Thomas, and Thomas was happy because he had seen Jesus and he knew for himself that Jesus was alive.

Sometimes Thomas gets called Doubting Thomas because he wouldn't believe his friends that Jesus was alive. That seems a bit unfair to me because the Bible also tells us that the other friends of Jesus were doubters too. They didn't believe the women who had found Jesus' tomb empty. But that's another story.

Ruth Burgess, Spill the Beans

Thomas was always late

Thomas was always late.

Sometimes he got up late.
Sometimes he forgot the time.
Sometimes he forgot where he was supposed to be.

All the friends of Jesus had been together last week
and Thomas was supposed to be with them
and he forgot.

Sometimes it didn't matter if Thomas was late,
but this time it did.

Jesus had met with his friends,
and talked to them,
and they were all happy
and Thomas had missed it.

Thomas was sad
that he had missed seeing Jesus.

'Maybe Jesus will come again next week,'
thought Thomas.
'I'm going to try and be there.'

Thomas thought up all kinds of ways to remind himself to be there.

He wrote in the dust on his table – 'don't be late!'
but his cat rolled over and over on the table purring
and rubbed the message away.

He tied a knot in his hankie,
but then he lost his hankie –
so that wasn't much help!

He asked his brother to remind him,
but his brother went away on a journey,
so that didn't help either.

Thomas said it over and over in his head:
'Don't be late to see Jesus.
Don't be late to see Jesus.
Don't be late to see Jesus.
Don't be late to see Jesus.'

He hoped and hoped he wouldn't forget.

And he didn't.

The next week when Jesus came again to talk to his friends
Thomas was there.
He'd made it!

He was so pleased to see Jesus.
and Jesus was pleased to see him.

You know
Thomas is still late for things sometimes
but not as late as he used to be.
He doesn't want to miss seeing Jesus or his friends.

Ruth Burgess, Spill the Beans

Flesh, blood, bones

The widow comes up the hill each morning to bring me food, and sweep the floor and take my clothes to wash. Sometimes her grandson comes and plays with the roughly carved wooden creatures that I have whittled. We talk together, comfortable under the fig tree in the yard, and he plays at our feet. She brings me news from the village and from the harbour, where the transport galleys call in with reminders of that vast and distant empire. Sometimes a new garrison guard comes clashing onto the stones of the quayside and the old one leaves, relieved to abandon the quiet and tedium of their posting. There, under the brilliant blue of the sky, cargo boats and fishing vessels nudge the quay. Her news stirs old memories, and I can feel the sea shifting and swelling beneath the bottom of the boat and the rough pull of the ropes and I seem to see the glittering slither of the catch of fish.

When she has gone, mostly I am alone, save for the weekly visit of some bored soldier from the camp, men who are sometimes eager for a different face and voice, sometimes gruff with the frustration of this edge-of-empire posting, an exile for them as well as for me. Yet I am not alone, when every waking moment crowds with memories, voices, pangs of emotion, the sure hope of reunion. My mind is filled with images, echoes, words that come striding out of the past to startle me afresh, as they did then. Sometimes my dreams are filled with dread; with wings, flames, chariots, blood, thunder, and I write of things to come, of a future hidden in secrets that speak to the unendurable present. But mostly now I seek the shade and silence, my body eased and my mind quietened, and let my memory drift as the sea will take it.

I know that soon all this will fade from me, not into forgetfulness, but with the slow withdrawal of the senses: taste and scent, sight and hearing. Only touch will accompany me at the last, and then, after I have fallen asleep, it will most truly awaken me to life, to the grip of that eternal embrace.

But touch. It is of that that I am thinking as I write this letter to you. Touch, and sight, and sound. Those things tell us truly that we know without doubt. The evidence. The substance. The fact. I did not see the pattern when I first began to write. I was too caught up with the story, with the need to take my friend through that salvaging conversation in the sealed room where we hid. A conversation so painful in its honesty, yet so healing in its truth. I did not see then, as I see now, as I begin this letter to you, my dear children, that it was the great climax of those days and weeks.

I often wonder where he went, Thomas. Strange, we never spoke of it, not even in the celebration and outburst of faith that followed. None of us spoke of those three days: the terrible first evening; then the Sabbath that confined us within the strictures of the Law and held us motionless with shame and horror; and at last the dawn and its aftermath and the slow gathering of extraordinary news all through that day. I do not know where he went. Some of us huddled together, with the women, hiding behind locked doors in Jerusalem. Others scattered, running as far as they could reach before the Sabbath held them still. Perhaps he went to the sisters in Bethany. They would have taken him in and cared for him. Perhaps: I don't know. But I imagine him stumbling blindly from Jerusalem, sleeping in a grove of olives and weeping alone, hiding through all the hours of Sabbath until he felt compelled to return long after noon on the first day of the week, only to find us gabbling the news with starting eyes and tongues that seemed too slow to tell of the sudden wonder.

Thomas. We knew him back in the early days, son of the boat builder in Capernaum, just a little distance from our own town on the shores of the lake. Fishermen need to trust the skill of the men who build their boats. Sound tackle, watertight planking, trimness of steering and buoyancy in waves that can turn in an instant from serenity to vicious lashing tumult in a squall. We saw that often enough, and once with the Master asleep in the stern and the boat ready to capsize. Yet Thomas, gripping the ropes, his feet wide-planted on the boards, Thomas determined to rely on the soundness of the boat, to trust to the evidence of his hands and feet, to the skill of his craft as a boat builder, while we panicked around him and woke up the Lord to save us. Evidence. Substance. His faith rested on it. His survival. I don't think we understood him then. I understand a little now, looking back on the things he said, the questions he asked. Building boats to take men safely on the surface of the water; to carry them from their natural home of the land into that other element: ruthless, fickle, beautiful, fecund, unnatural: the sea. Always test the evidence; prove the soundness of the vessel. You cannot entrust your life to an uncertain boat. Matthew Levi, who was (if any of us were) closer to him than anyone else, was much the same in his demand for certainty, for proof. Philip too.

None of us really understood. We saw miracles, yes, we saw with our own eyes things happen to flesh and blood. But those mysterious, awful words spoken in the months while we slowly journeyed nearer to Jerusalem. We didn't comprehend and struggled to stay in a place of reality.

'You will die,' we said.

'Yes,' he would answer. 'Yes. I tell you the truth. That is what I must do.'

It was Thomas who saw the inevitability of death even as we travelled to awaken Lazarus. 'Let us go and die with him,' he said.

There is one other thing about Thomas that we failed to grasp in those days, even though it defined him. We called him 'Twin'. A name from birth, a nickname but also a name. Not a name given to both, but only to one, the surviving one. The younger died, he once said, within hours of his birth. It cast a shade on the living, and Thomas felt always alone, separated, I think, as if he must live for both, as if his life had been paid for by his brother. Always in the shadow of death. So when he said, 'Lord, we don't know where you are going. How can we know the way?' It was out of great anguish of heart. He had lived all his life in that great unknowing. And then that great and terrible dying, crushing him with grief and despair. Survival at the expense of another. Abandonment. The shame of fleeing away after the arrest.

As I said, I do not know, and will never know now, where he went and whether he found any comfort or solace.

But he came back, long after the heat of noon had passed on that first day of the week. And we were like men in a high fever, delirious, laughing, weeping with relief, incoherent; babbling of visits to the tomb and appearances to the women and then to Peter. And others too, came with their story that evening, but Thomas had gone. Later that night, I remember, the Lord came to us and in our excitement and hope and terror we thought he was a vision or a ghost, until he spoke familiar words to us and showed us the wounds of his hands and feet. We clung to one another, growing in confidence and faith as we repeated the stories, remembering what we had been taught. Thomas, drawn almost against his will, revisited us early in the week, but shrugged at our stories.

'Unless I see, and touch, I will not believe,' he said.

As I think of him now, so many years after those hectic days of celebration, I say to you, do not judge him, and call it doubt. Here was a man who knew too well that you cannot entrust your life to an uncertain vessel. You cannot move into a different element unless you know that your boat is sound. A man who had lived all his life in the knowledge that death steals from you, had stolen from him half his very self, his womb brother. Do you not think that Jesus knew that and heard what lay behind that desperate plea for evidence? A week later, and Thomas was with us (where else could he go?), and he saw with his own eyes, heard the true voice, was invited to touch and know. It was Thomas who broke through then with greater understanding than any of us.

'My Lord and my God,' he said.

He saw what we were still slow to see, that this Man, this Word made flesh, was the incarnate God. God in substance, in humanity, flesh and blood and bones, fully human, fully God, and death will be no more. And every tear will be wiped from our eyes and we shall see him clearly and all our mourning will be forever over.

And so I write to you now, long, long after those days of crisis and despair, hope and joy. As I write, I remember him, Thomas, who grasped that truth instantly, completely, as I have, but long after. I do not know whether he still lives, only that he travelled east. He was older than I, and I am a very old man now. But soon I will know with complete certainty. So as I write to you, I tell you of a glory that we saw with our own eyes: the glory of God. And he lived with us, friend with friends, laughter with laughter, tears with tears, death with our death, life for our life. And we heard him and saw him, and our hands touched him.

I testify to this, my dear children. Now, as I come near to the end of my life, I testify to you, remembering Thomas, and the completeness of his joy.

Janet Killeen

Late that evening
(John 20:19–29)

(Tune: 'The burning of Auchindoun', Scots traditional)

Late that evening
ten disciples gathered,
fearful who might drag them
to the governor or priests.
As they waited,
doors fast-bolted,
Jesus stood among them,
saying softly, 'Be at peace.'

'As God sent me,
so I send you;
feel the Father's life in you,
and breathe his living breath.
By his Spirit
breathe forgiveness;
heaven purges guilt
that is forgiven here on earth.'

Thomas doubted:
'Till I touch him,
sense and reason
will not be denied.'
One week after,
as they gathered,
Jesus came, and answered:
'Thomas, touch my hands and side.'

Heaven blesses
those who saw him,
trusting what their eyes revealed
in spite of all they knew.
Then what blessing
guides their spirits –
those who neither saw nor touched
but trust the word is true.

Roddy Cowie

See: https://soundcloud.com/roddy-6/doubting-thomas

Looking back
(John 21:1–14)

Looking back
it was strange really.
But maybe it wasn't.
We were back where it had all started for us,
back by the sea of Galilee,
and Peter was going fishing,
and we were going with him.

There were seven of us,
seven disciples of Jesus:
Peter and James and John,
Nathanael and Thomas
and me and one of the others.

It was good to be back in the boat,
back on the lake,
back doing something familiar.
Although we'd dropped the nets
a few times that night
the fish had evaded us.
Day was just breaking
and we'd decided to head for the shore.

Someone shouted to us from the shore.
He'd obviously had better luck than us:
we could smell fish cooking.
It smelt good.
Maybe he was going to invite us to share his breakfast.

As we got nearer we could hear what he was saying.
He told us to let down our nets on the right side of the boat.
We did – and the net filled so quickly
that although there were seven of us
we could not haul it on board.

John said to Peter,
'It's Jesus!'
And Peter,
impetuous as ever,
jumped into the lake
and swam and paddled to the shore.

We brought the boat in slowly;
we didn't want to lose the catch –
some of the fish were huge.
We counted them later;
there were 153 of them.
Not bad for a long night
and a few frantic moments at daybreak.

Jesus had the fish we'd smelt
cooking on charcoal;
he had bread too
and he invited us to
come and have breakfast
and we did.

Looking back
it was strange really,
being back where he had invited us to follow him,
but maybe it wasn't.

Maybe he knew that
our ordinary lives,
our working, our sharing food,
our disappointments, our joys,
our questions, our wonder,
were the experiences in which we needed to recognise him,
needed to know that he would always be with us.

Ruth Burgess, Spill the Beans

One, two, three, four

(John 21:1–14)

One, two, three, four,
that's four fish, big ones, that I've just pulled out of the net.

Five, six, seven, eight, nine ... two of them are enormous;
ten, eleven, twelve, thirteen ...
let me tell you how we caught them.
There were seven of us
and we'd gone out for a night's fishing in Peter's boat.
Fish are sometimes easier to catch at night;
they're curious;
if you hold a lamp over the water
they'll come up to see what's going on.

Fourteen, fifteen, sixteen, seventeen, eighteen,
anyway, we'd fished all night,
put the net down a few times
and caught nothing – not even an old piece of rope!

Nineteen, twenty, let's count in twos for a bit,
twenty-two, twenty-four, twenty-six ...
we could see that it was nearly dawn,
bit of light in the sky, in the east,
and we heard someone shouting.

Twenty-eight, thirty, thirty-two, thirty-four, thirty-six, thirty-eight,
we couldn't make out the words at first,
the person was too far away.

Forty, still loads of fish to count, let's count in fives,
forty-five, fifty, fifty-five, sixty, sixty-five ...
As we got closer we could hear more clearly.
It was a man's voice and he told us to drop our net
to the right side of the boat;
we'd caught nothing all night,
but maybe he could see something that we couldn't;
it was worth a chance.

Seventy, seventy-five, eighty, eighty-five –
it was amazing, the net filled up straight away with fish,
these fish I'm counting now,
and John suddenly shouted to Peter: 'It's Jesus!'
and Peter jumped out of the boat and swam and paddled to the shore.

Ninety, ninety-five, one hundred, let's count in tens,
one hundred and ten, one hundred and twenty …
the rest of us brought the boat in slowly,
we didn't want to lose our catch.
As we neared the shore we could smell fish cooking.
Jesus must have had better luck than us last night,
he was cooking breakfast.

One hundred and thirty, one hundred and forty, need to go slower now,
I've nearly counted all of them. They're very slippery …
one hundred and forty-two, one hundred and forty-four,
one hundred and forty-six, one hundred and forty-seven,
one hundred and forty-eight, one hundred and forty-nine …
So here I am, counting all the fish we've caught.
I like counting.

One hundred and fifty,
whoops, dropped one,
one hundred and fifty-one –
the fish on the barbecue smells great!
Looks like Jesus has caught enough for all of us,
he's got some bread too,
thinks of everything.

One hundred and fifty-two, last one,
one hundred and fifty-three.
What a catch!
We're going to have a great day at the market.
But first,
it's time for breakfast.

Ruth Burgess, Spill the Beans

Note: You might need a signal to stop counting when telling this story. With older children you could make the counting more complicated, e.g. count in threes or sevens …

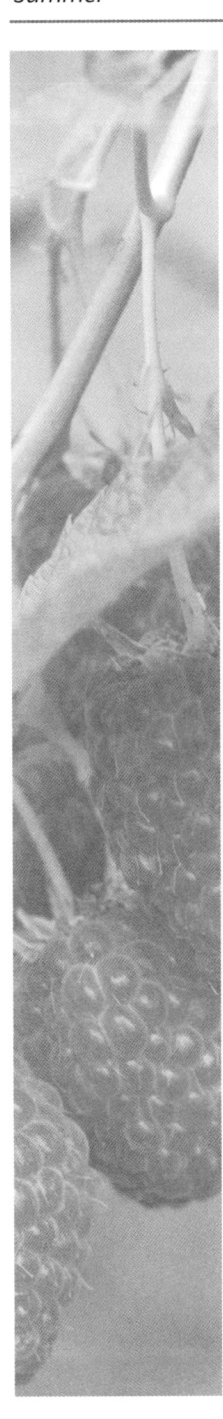

Anchovy and zebra fish

You could do this by encouraging members of the congregation to call out a fish species for each letter of the alphabet, while keeping this list yourself for those tricky letters.

Anchovy,
Bass,
Cod,
Dogfish,
Eel,
Flounder,
Guppy,
Herring,
Icefish,
Javelin,
Koi,
Lamprey,
Mackerel,
Needlefish,
Opah,
Plaice,
Quillback,
Ray,
Salmon,
Tuna,
Uaru,
Velvetfish,
Whiting,
X-ray fish,
Yellowtail,
Zebrafish.

Such an abundance of variety,
all part of your wondrous creation,
shared with us.

May we recognise amongst us too
that same wonderful variety
of people.

We are all different,
but we all have our own special gifts,
and all of us are loved by God.
Amen

Peter Johnston, Spill the Beans

The fisher-folk of this world

You can change this to suit your own locale.

Lord of the water,
of North Sea and Clyde,
of Forth and Tay,
of Loch Lomond and Loch Fyne,
of the Red Sea and Galilean Lake,
today we pray for the fisher-folk of this world
who make their living from the sea.
At times dangerous
often with no guarantee of a catch,
or a decent price at market;
challenging,
the separation from loved ones
sometimes taking its toll.

We pray for communities
where once a decent living
could be expected
for generation upon generation of fisher-folk,
who today suffer unemployment and wider problems.

We pray for the marine scientists and conservationists
who look after our waterways and oceans.

For campaigners who take seriously the cleanliness of our oceans
and work for a plastic-free environment
for the living organisms of our seas.

We pray for those who endure drought,
whose rivers have dried up,
for those whose crops have failed
and where food shortages mean starving people.

We remember those who live in villages
where the well has dried up,
and people who must travel miles
to get the water they need.

Lord of creation,
may it rain where there is drought;
and where there is flooding may the waters recede.
May your grace and mercy flood this world,
and may your abundant blessing of love
never be hindered by our greed.
In Jesus' name we pray.
Amen

Keith Blackwood, Spill the Beans

I'm going fishing

(Tune: 'Long Cookstown/Nancy Whiskey', Irish traditional)

Said Simon Peter, 'I'm going fishing.'
'Then we'll come with you,' said all the rest.
They took the boat, and all night they laboured
and yet by dawn they had empty nets.
But then a voice from the shoreline called them:
'I see the fish have been hard to find
but throw your net now a bit to starboard.'
The weight of fish nearly broke their lines.

Said John to Peter, 'It must be Jesus.'
And in an instant he grabbed his coat
and swam for shore while the others fumbled,
then slowly, slowly brought in the boat.
And when they landed, a fire was burning,
and cooking on it, some fish and bread.
'Bring up the fish that you caught this morning,
we'll eat like royalty,' Jesus said.

He called them round and he gave them breakfast.
They saw the way that he broke the bread.
They all remembered another lakeside –
and knew the one they were sure was dead.
Then after breakfast he beckoned Peter,
'You say you love me, but is it true?'
'Oh yes,' said Peter, 'you surely know it.'
'Then feed my lambs just as I would do.'

Three times he asked it, and Peter answered
as three times Peter had once denied.
He walked ahead then, and Peter followed
and John walked close on the other side.
It was by John that the words were written;
he testified that the tale was true –
and all he wrote was a tiny portion
of what his eyes saw his master do.

Roddy Cowie

Down-under resurrection

Jesus,
it must have been a relief
to escape the searing heat
of vicious tongues
and pain of piercing nails,
and to rest in the dark tomb.
And then there was the wetness
of the dewy grass under your feet
in the garden.
And here you are now
on the seashore,
feeling the coolness
of the sand between your toes.
Now,
with all that renewed energy,
I don't suppose you're up for
a game of beach cricket?

Sr Sandra Sears, CSBC

Breakfast on the shore
(John 21:15–25)

Breakfast.
Breakfast on the seashore with Jesus.
We'd always enjoyed breakfast, before the day got busy
with the crowd's demands and questions.

That last time,
after we'd been fishing all night
and caught nothing,
and then he'd shouted to us from the shore at daybreak
to put our nets down and they'd filled with fish,
that last time,

when he had fish cooking on the charcoal
and fresh bread –
that was a great breakfast.

After that breakfast, Jesus had a long talk with Peter.
I don't know if Peter realised then
that he would end up being a leader in the early church,
that people would gossip about his lack of education,
and remember that he had denied Jesus in the Temple courtyard,
that people would be critical of his behaviour.

Whatever Jesus said to Peter,
and Peter told us a bit about their conversation afterwards,
it was enough to convince Peter
that Jesus still loved him and believed in him
and had a job for him to do.

Jesus also dealt with the rumour
going the rounds about one of us
not dying until he comes again.
He said rumours about what's going to happen to other people
should not be our concern:
our task is to tell other people
about his life and love.

And so
this is the end of my book.
I've tried to write down for you
everything I know about Jesus.
There are lots of other things Jesus did –
if they were all written down one by one
I don't suppose the whole world
would be able to hold
all the books that would be written about him!

Ruth Burgess, Spill the Beans

All those slippery fish

(John 21:15–25)

Remember last week,
I was on the shore
counting all those slippery fish,
one, two, three, four …
all the way up to one hundred and fifty-three of them?

And then I went to have breakfast with Jesus.
It was a great breakfast,
fish grilled on charcoal
and fresh bread,
maybe not what you usually eat for breakfast,
but we were hungry, we'd been working all night,
and we really enjoyed it.

After breakfast Jesus had a long talk with Peter.
You might remember that the night before Jesus was killed
Peter had said three times in the Temple courtyard
that he didn't know Jesus.
Well, I think that Jesus was giving Peter a chance to put that right.
Peter told us afterwards that Jesus had asked him three times
if he loved him
and when Peter had told Jesus three times that of course he loved him,
Jesus told Peter that he was to look after people
and care for them, like shepherds care for their sheep.

Peter became a leader in the early church
and Jesus knew that that would happen.
I think Jesus wanted Peter to know
that even when people make mistakes
he would always love them and be close to them.

In the years that followed our breakfast on the beach with Jesus,
we all tried to keep on doing what Jesus had told us to do.
Someone thought that it would be a good idea to write down
what Jesus had said and done,
and we did our best to remember Jesus' stories

and the people he met.
Mary was still alive
and she could remember what Jesus was like as a boy,
and Peter and Andrew remembered Jesus first calling them to follow him.

I don't suppose we remembered everything,
and even if we did –
there wouldn't be room enough in the world
for all the books that would be written.

Ruth, Burgess, Spill the Beans

Some doubted

(Matthew 28:16–20)

I sometimes wonder if the church has a place
for people who are like me.
Everybody else seems to know their Bible better than I do,
and I was never any good
at those memory verse things as a child.

Not only do I feel like a second-class Christian,
but my faith is so fragile, weak,
compared to other people in our church.

I doubt myself all the time,
and I wonder about all those miracles Jesus performed,
whether they could really have happened.

People don't want to hear about my doubts.

They want the right answer,
the straightforward facts,
the truth as the minister or the church sees it,
and they go about their business
feeling assured, confident, Christ-like.

That is why I hide a lot when it comes to things in our church.
I never go to those Bible study or house-groups
in case people think I am just a fake Christian.

I never turn up at the prayer group,
because I don't think I could pray in front of other people,
and Mrs Barrie is so eloquent when she prays
that it puts you to shame.
I am not as well-educated as her,
so I doubt that God would even take the time
to listen to anything I had to say or ask.

Yet every so often I am encouraged,
and feel that even if the church, the Holy Willies or the minister
might not think much of me,
because of my doubts,
I know that Jesus still finds a place for me.
He still thinks that I belong,
fragile and weak though I am.

Here, even amidst the joy of Easter,
the Good News of resurrection and life,
some doubted,
but were nevertheless encouraged
to go and live what they believed,
act on what they believed,
grow into what God might like them to become,
with their doubts and their mustard-seed faith,
and still find their place amongst God's cherished ones.

Today I want to feel affirmed in who I am,
what I am able to believe,
what I might become,
because I believe that God
is not finished with me yet.

So I will go and teach
what I know,
what I have already experienced,
what I am able to believe,
and trust that God will do the rest.

Spill the Beans

Easter is ...

Easter is ...

Easter is when Jesus' friends are happy.
Easter is when the Easter bunny comes.
Easter is when my mum won't tell me where she's hidden the Easter eggs.
Easter is nice and good children.
Easter is decorating eggs.
Easter is when my sister eats my Easter eggs because I don't like chocolate.
Easter is when Jesus was brave.
Easter is finding eggs in the wash house.
Easter is when you get up early and eat all day.
Easter is when we go yummy for eggs.
Easter is getting fat.
Easter is when the stone moved.
Easter is starting a new life for baby chicks.
Easter is when you dance about.
Easter is when Jesus came back alive.
Easter is sharing eggs.
Easter is when we get lots of surprises.

A class of seven-year-olds

When flowers bloom

(Opening responses for Eastertide)

When flowers bloom in the desert,
Christ is risen.
Alleluia, Alleluia!

When enemies sit around tables and talk about peace,
Christ is risen.
Alleluia, Alleluia!

When people stand up for what is right in the face of great evil,
Christ is risen.
Alleluia, Alleluia!

When, despite hardship and struggle, people sing and dance,
Christ is risen.
Alleluia, Alleluia!

When prison bars are shattered
by the cry of
'Freedom!',
Christ is risen.
Alleluia, Alleluia!

When in our wounded and broken world,
life triumphs over death,
peace over war,
hope over fear,
freedom over captivity,
love over hate,
Christ is risen.
He is risen indeed.
Alleluia, Alleluia!

Liz Delafield

The birds sang

(An Easter litany)

The birds sang
alleluias were freed
the disciples ran
dawn slipped in
the garden woke
the mountains quaked
the tomb rocked
and the stone rolled.

Light exploded
time held its breath
the women wept
the gardener spoke
the angels danced
the world woke
the tomb rocked
and the stone rolled.

The stars rejoiced
the sun bowed
the Spirit laughed
the water flowed
the bread broke
the wine shimmered
the tomb rocked
and the stone rolled.

Zacchaeus winked
Mary cried
Bartimaeus saw
the leper danced
the prodigal came home
the lost sheep was found
the tomb rocked
and the stone rolled.

Mustard grew
the cripple walked
poor were blessed
peacemakers made peace
the storm calmed
cheeks were turned
the tomb rocked
and the stone rolled.

The time is now
the place is here
the people are us
the word is spoken
the Son is alive
the Resurrection is true
the tomb rocks
and the stone rolls.

John Murning, Spill the Beans

Let us say that again

'Living God!'
Let us say that again:
'Living God!'

May the life you have redeemed
from death
be alive in us,
that in our living and being
we proclaim
a life that never dies –
and is so full of alleluias
of the love of justice
and the making of peace,
it can never die.

May we find a million ways
to proclaim you are alive:
in word and deed,
in hope and action,
in longing and being,
in singing and speaking,
in laughter and care,
in questions and wonder,
in faith and belief.

May we be your resurrection people,
alive to life
and ready to share it
with the world.

Hear us,
live in us,
reshape us,
call us
anew
and again
into life
and all its fullness.
So be it.

Roddy Hamilton, Spill the Beans

Easter in spite of myself

On a day when I struggle to get out of bed,
and long to walk any path but the one you have set before me,
I trudge to the river with my four-legged companion
who must and will be walked.

It is then that I see, as if for the first time, the beauty of this place:
sunlight on the water,
birdsong all around
and a pervading sense of peace.

And I experience footsteps in the dew,
and a voice calls my name
and I know in the depth of my being
that you have arisen and once more it is Easter in my heart.

Elizabeth Clark

From the dark mornings

From the dark mornings of depression you call us.
You call us into being once again,
giving us the chance to find our true selves,
renewing us from inside out.

You believed in us
throughout that long fearful journey.
You, O God, gave us the chance to start again:
the gift of new life,
the gift of being happy to be alive.

Thank you, God, for this new day.
Thank you, God, that I can pray.
Thank you for the sun's rising.
Thank you that I'm more than surviving.

Katy Owen

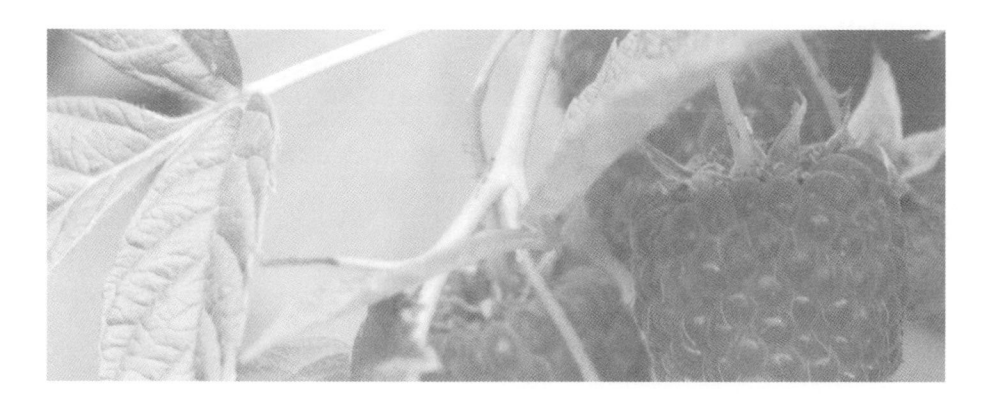

Easter paths

The Resurrection changes everything.
It is an invitation to live differently.
To make a difference.
It is the source of hope, life and faith for Jesus' followers.
It is a challenge
to let new ways of behaving
and believing emerge.
It creates a kaleidoscope of different
styles of life,
patterns of belief
and rhythms of worship.
The God of Resurrection
brings life from death,
hope from despair,
new disconcerting paths to explore.

They are paths of transformation –
from fear to trust, from the known to the unknown,
from disappointment to delight, from stay to go,
from blame to forgiveness, from here to infinity
and from condemnation to encounter.

The path of tears

Mary weeps.
They are the tears of grief and longing.
Tears respond to what words cannot describe.
They speak of pathways of experience deep within us.

The path of doubt

Thomas, the lonely disciple.
He spoke what others only thought.
He never felt the others were comfortable with that.
Thomas, the missing disciple.
He needed time to himself.

He needed time with his questions.
They were not ready for public consumption.
Thomas, the isolated disciple.
He was given a special invitation from Jesus.

The path of disappointment

They have no name.
But their struggle with Christ is familiar.
He is not what we thought.
He has to meet us in another way.

The path of failure

Peter and Jesus met on a beach.
Nothing was said about what had happened.
Past failings cannot be removed from the record.
Redemption was offered – through a tough choice.

The path of disorientation

Paul had a faith and he was happy with it.
Then came a moment it could not contain.
He could no longer see his way ahead.
The old would become the birthplace of the new.

So!
God, you are present in the familiar and secure.
When we run for cover because we are tired
or too anxious to face disappointment or loss,
draw us out of fright and uncertainty
and stand with us in strength and power.

John Rackley

Partners and co-workers

Is God good news for women?
Could Jesus have fulfilled his earthly ministry without women?
God needed women to be his partners and co-workers
in his plan to reveal himself to humanity.

Without Elizabeth, prepared to risk the hazards of childbirth in old age,
there would have been no forerunner,
no John the Baptist to prepare the way.

Without Mary, prepared to be humiliated
by bearing a child outside of marriage,
there would have been no God-made-man,
no Emmanuel to bear our sins and reunite humanity to God.

Without Peter's mother-in-law, prepared to offer her home,
there would have been no focal point,
no home for Jesus to rest.

Without the women who followed him,
Joanna, Susanna and numerous Marys prepared to give up lives to care,
there would have been no one to attend to Jesus' human needs.

Without the woman, prepared to risk her reputation,
prepared to give all her wealth,
there would have been no one to anoint Jesus for burial,
to bring dignity to the body sacrificed to reconcile humanity to God.

Without the women of Jerusalem, weeping on the way to the cross,
there would have been no one to mourn,
no one to weep for Christ on his way to save the world.

Without Mary Magdalene, prepared to rise early and go to the tomb,
how long would the world have waited to hear of the Resurrection?
And would the Ascension ever have been understood?

And what of those who went before?
Sarah, Rachel, Leah and Rebecca,
Tamar, Rahab, Ruth and Naomi,
Deborah, Bathsheba, Esther and Gomer.
Many others, recorded and unrecorded,
faithful to the God of Abraham, Isaac and Jacob,
the God of Sarah, Rachel and Rebecca.
Without their faithfulness,
there would have been no possibility of God revealing himself as a child.

And what of those who have come since –
Priscilla, Junia, Eunice and Tryphena –
of the countless millions down the centuries?
Without them being prepared to lift their heads
to name themselves the daughters of God,
who would have cared in the name of Christ,
and made him known to many?

And so God is good news for women.
God needs women to be his partners and co-workers.
Women who will stand up with dignity and courage.
Daughters, loved and chosen by God,
to share in His work in the world.
Not because God is small and weak,
unable to act without women,
but because God created women in his own image.
Because he chooses to work with women to reveal himself to humanity.
God is good news for women.

S Anne Lawson

The hope in our hearts

'What is Easter?' they ask.
It belongs to the life and love;
it follows the healing and welcome;
it echoes the upturning of tables
and the peacemaking.
It summarises the blessing
on the mount and the breaking
of bread.

Then there's the cross and its agony;
three days later an empty tomb;
broken bread and fish on the shore;
the mystery of the resurrection
and the turning from despair
to the joy of new beginnings;
new beginnings that we share today.

'What is Easter?' they ask.
It's about the collapse of a wall,
the building of a clinic.
It leads the way to the child
who now walks, the old woman
who can see again,
the bomb that didn't fall,
the clasp of hands, black and brown.
It spells the hope in our hearts,
the glory of reds and yellows in spring,

a gift exploding into a new day,
a gong sounding over and over in ecstasy,
the past crashing into the present,
the present opening doors to eternity.

Judy Dinnen

Stories from the
Acts of the Apostles

Dear Theophilus

(Acts 1:1–14)

Dear Theophilus,

My second book! Wow!

The first one, as you know, was all about Jesus. Who he was. What he taught. The stories he told. The people he met. His friends and enemies. The women who looked out for him. How he died. How he came back from death and met his friends.

You remember where I finished the last book? I told you about Jesus meeting those two people walking to Emmaus and how at first they didn't recognise him, and then, when he broke bread with them – they realised who he was.

And I told you how the disciples thought Jesus was a ghost, and then he asked them for food. What kind of a ghost eats food?!

I told you how Jesus reminded the disciples about what would happen to him, and how he would come back from death and be with them.

And then I wrote a little bit about Jesus going to heaven, and I had to finish because there was no more room on the scroll.

But now, Theophilus, Book Two. I had to write it because after Jesus went back to heaven all sorts of exciting things began to happen to the disciples. Jesus was still with them; even if they couldn't see him any more they knew he was there. And they began to do some of the things that Jesus had done. They told people about God, they met angels, they shared their stories and their food, they listened to women and respected them, they healed people.

But I'm getting ahead of myself. I want to start this book with the story of Jesus being taken into heaven and tell you a bit more about it.

After that Sunday morning when Jesus met the women at the tomb, Jesus met with his disciples many times over the next forty days. He told them that they needed to stay in Jerusalem and that after he had gone back to be with his Father, they would discover that he was with them in a new way.

Stories from the Acts of the Apostles   81

The disciples, as always, were full of questions, and Jesus kept on telling them that after he had left them they would travel to distant lands to tell people all about him. It was exciting and scary all at the same time.

And then Jesus left them. They found it hard to describe. They said it was as if a cloud surrounded him and he disappeared. And they saw two men, who talked to them about Jesus. Maybe it was the same men who the women had met at the tomb? Maybe those men were angels? Who knows?

And after that, they all went back to Jerusalem. And they stayed together – the disciples, Mary the mother of Jesus, Jesus' brothers and the women who were close to Jesus. And they shared their food and they talked and they prayed.

O Theophilus, you'll find it hard to believe what happened next. I think I'm going to call Book Two 'the dispersal of the disciples' – or maybe 'the Acts of the Apostles' – it's amazing stuff!

Ruth Burgess, Spill the Beans

Ben's stories

(Acts 1:1–14)

Ben liked writing. He enjoyed keeping a diary. He liked writing stories at school. He liked writing letters to his granny. He even liked writing thank you letters to the people who sent him presents for his birthday.

Ben liked words. He liked words that made sounds – words like sizzle and woof and splash. He enjoyed learning long words – words that he found in the dictionary – words like calamity and whipper-snapper. Ben liked rhyming words, words like clock and dock and sock. He loved words that had a tune to go with them; he knew lots of songs. And Ben enjoyed playing games with words. He often played Scrabble with his friends – and he was very good at it.

Ben wasn't sure what he wanted to be when he grew up but he knew that he wanted to do something that involved writing and words. Perhaps he could be a journalist and be sent to find news stories and write them up for the newspapers.

You could talk with the children about writing stories.

Perhaps he could write plays and they would be performed in theatres. Maybe he could write a long story and it could be made into a book and his name would be on the cover. Perhaps he could write a song, but he would need to find somebody else to help him write a tune.

Ben sometimes read about other writers. There was a man called Samuel Pepys who had kept a diary, and reading it now helped people to know about the great fire of London in 1666. And there were the Brontë sisters who lived in Yorkshire and wrote novels. And he'd watched a programme on the television about James Barrie, who'd written the story *Peter Pan*.

In Sunday school Ben learned about the people who wrote down the books and stories in the Bible. One of them was called Luke. Some people thought Luke was a doctor and that he travelled with Saint Paul.

Ben liked Luke's story of Jesus. It was Luke who wrote down some of the stories about Jesus' birth, the stories about the shepherds and the inn. Luke's story of Jesus includes lots of the stories Jesus told. Without Luke's book no one would know about the Good Samaritan or the lost coin or the two brothers. It was Luke who wrote down the stories of Paul's travels and what happened in the early church.

St Luke's books are famous. People enjoy reading them. One day Ben might write a book or a song or a play. He might become a games-maker or a poet or a journalist. One day Ben might be famous too.

Ruth Burgess, Spill the Beans

Home visit

(Acts 3:1–10)

Peter: John?

John: Yes, Peter.

Peter: What happened?

John: What happened?

Peter: What happened in the Temple this afternoon?

John: Peter, you know what happened. You spoke to a lame man who was begging at the Temple gate, and you told him, in the name of Jesus, to get up and walk, and you pulled him to his feet and he was healed.

Peter: I know all that, John – it was amazing. Everyone who knew the man and saw him walking around in the Temple was amazed as well. But, John, what happened?

John: Peter, what do you mean? What are you asking?

Peter: John, what's happening to me? To us? How come that man was healed? What's going on?

John: Peter, do you remember what happened to us on the day of Pentecost and how you stood up and talked to the crowds about Jesus and how people believed in him and were baptised?

Peter: I remember. I never thought I could stand up and speak like that, but I did.

John: You did, and you did it because something inside you helped you to do it.

Peter: Go on.

John: Jesus told us that he would always be with us, and somehow he is. It's like he's inside us and he's as real to us as he was before he died. It was Jesus who healed that man this afternoon and he did it using

>   your voice and your hands. Jesus is still with us, Peter, with you, with me, with all of us. That's what's going on!
>
> *Peter:* Wow! You really think so?
>
> *John:* You know, Peter, I think that Jesus is really enjoying all this!
>
> *Peter:* Enjoying?
>
> *John:* Enjoying seeing us do things that he did, enjoying us finding out how God's love works in us, enjoying listening to our questions and our prayers.
>
> *Peter:* You know, John, part of me misses the Jesus who was beside us before he died. I miss his smile, his jokes, his tears, his anger and his stories – I miss all that – and yet the way I know that Jesus is close to me now, giving me hope and strength and love, well, he feels closer than ever.
>
> *John:* I know what you mean, Peter, and I think Jesus is really smiling now. You know, none of us ever imagined you turning into a theologian!
>
> **Ruth Burgess, Spill the Beans**

Be healed

(Acts 3:1–10)

'BE HEALED IN THE NAME OF JESUS!'
'Be healed!'
Just like that!
In an instant,
like the flick of a switch, the turn of a page.
Just … like … that.
Be healed.

And yet I know folk who have not been healed;
not instantly anyway.
I know that in my body and mind and spirit and heart
many a time I am not healed;

not all at once anyway.
Not the TV healing
in exciting and bold and dramatic ways.

Yet it does happen: healing.
I know it.
I have seen it.
As the clock tick-tocks:
as moments turn to minutes,
minutes turn to hours,
hours to days,
days to weeks,
weeks to months,
months to years.
It can take time to heal
and we can heal in time.
And the God of eternity
who holds all time
and all souls
and all power
in his hands …
the living God heals.

Dramatically.
Quietly.
Powerfully.
Peacefully.

Pause

Be healed in the name of Jesus.

Scott Burton, Spill the Beans

What did you expect?

(Based on Acts 3:1–10)

Cast:

Nathan
Tourist
Guide
Joe
Priest
Peter
John (non-speaking role)

Setting:

At the Beautiful Gate of the Temple in Jerusalem. Stage directions assume a typical church setting, with the main entrance behind the congregation, performance space in front and an aisle allowing movement between them. At the start, Nathan is sitting on the floor or leaning against a wall just inside the entrance. The Guide is at the front.

Nathan: *(to Tourist as s/he enters)* Spare a shekel? Thank you kindly. Enjoy your visit.

Tourist tries to be unobtrusive in taking a seat at the front.

Guide: Are you the last? Right, then I will begin. Welcome to Temple Tours. We are a large party today, so I will have to ask you to stay in your seats as I show you some of the features of this historic building. I will also introduce you to some of the characters who can be found here.

You will have an opportunity to ask questions, but please respect the local culture. While at first glance this may seem a rundown monument on the edge of our empire, to the people of this town – or city, as they like to call it – it represents the presence of their god.

Tourist: Well, in that case, they might tidy it up a bit. I nearly fell over a beggar as I came through the gate.

Guide: The gate is known as the Beautiful Gate, and I am afraid it is a popular pitch with beggars. You probably met Nathan – he's been there since I started these tours ten years ago. In fact, this man just coming in is one of the neighbours who carries him up in the mornings.

Joe enters, passing Nathan.

Nathan: Afternoon, Joe – say one for me when you're in there.

Tourist: Ask him why he can't stand on his own feet.

Guide: *(to Joe)* Excuse me. For the benefit of our overseas guests, could you tell us what is wrong with Nathan?

Joe: He's been lame from birth – midwife had a bad day, I gather. Never done more than drag himself around on his arms. But he's a cheerful soul, so we do our bit to help out.

Guide: And could you explain why you yourself have come to the Temple today?

Joe: This time of the afternoon is traditional for coming to pray – I don't come often, but when I do, I ask God to bless Nathan, as well as my family.

Tourist: What do you mean by 'bless'? Make us generous with our coins! I don't suppose your god would give him his legs back?

Joe: You'd have to ask the priests about that. In the old stories, I suppose God did do some amazing things, but we don't expect that nowadays. I just pay my respects to Him at the altar and hope to reach a quiet old age. Mind you, there have been some odd rumours in the city these last weeks – people saying one of the old prophets is back.

Guide: Ah, here is one of the priests, who will tell us about the faith and practice of the Temple.

Priest: Good afternoon, ladies and gentlemen. We welcome visitors of all nations to these outer courts of the Temple. This is an important heritage site, which is costly to maintain. You will find donation boxes on your way out. We do not permit non-believers to see the inner parts, where our rituals are held, but I can give you an outline. Our worship follows patterns which have been handed down over hundreds of years. There are detailed rules which our people follow about sacrificing anything from a pigeon to a bull to mark key points in the farming cycle and in their lives.

Tourist: Why?

Priest: It is written in our holy book.

Tourist: Yes, but why? Does anything change as a result?

Priest: Change? Why would we want that? Of course we do get people trying to stir things up, but we have ways of keeping them quiet. Only a few weeks ago … oh dear, those faces look familiar.

Nathan: *(to Peter and John as they enter at back)* Good afternoon, gentlemen – do I hear a northern accent? Welcome to Jerusalem. Could you spare a shekel?

Peter: My pockets are empty – but I will give you what I have. Look at me. Now take my hand.

Nathan: Who? … What? … Why? This is amazing – my legs are straightening – I can stand … I can run.

Nathan, Peter and John run to the front amid general praise and joy (except from priest), and draw Guide and Tourist into a dance.

Priest: *(to congregation)* Have you ever turned up for a quiet day at work and something totally unexpected messes it up?

All freeze.

Kit Walkham

The puzzling book
(Acts 8:26–39)

Have you ever tried to read something and found it really hard to understand?

There was once a man from Ethiopia who was travelling home in his horse and carriage, and on his way he was reading a book by a man called Isaiah. Isaiah was a friend of God, and he wrote lots of amazing things that he knew God wanted to say to people. But the man from Ethiopia found it all very puzzling and hard to understand. He read Isaiah's stories out loud to himself, as his horse trotted along and his carriage swayed from side to side. 'Oh dear,' thought the Ethiopian man, 'I wish someone could explain this book to me! It's so very hard to understand!' He sighed and went back to his reading, but try as he might, the stories in Isaiah's book just made no sense.

Just then, the Ethiopian man heard someone shouting out: 'What are you reading, my friend? Do you understand it?'

What a surprise for the Ethiopian man! He looked out of his carriage and saw another man running alongside him. So he pulled on the reins and made his horse and carriage stop. He welcomed his new friend up into the carriage and learned that his name was Philip.

Philip said, 'I see you're reading that wonderful book written by God's friend Isaiah. Do you understand the stories in it?'

The Ethiopian man laughed out loud. 'Oh, I wish I did! But no, I don't! How can I understand it when I've got no one to help me?'

'Well, I think I can help,' said Philip. 'Which bit are you stuck with?'

'Oh dear – I'm stuck with all of it!' said the Ethiopian, 'but let's start with this strange bit here … who is Isaiah talking about?' With that, he turned to the book and read aloud, '"Like a sheep he was led to be killed, and like a lamb that is silent before its wool is sheared, so he did not say a word".' The Ethiopian looked at Philip: 'What kind of person would behave like a sheep if someone was trying to kill them?' he asked. 'No wonder I can't understand it!'

'Well, it was just like that when Jesus died,' said Philip. 'People did terrible things to him and he was just like that quiet lamb, not saying a word.'

'Who is Jesus?' asked the Ethiopian.

Oh my – that got Philip talking! The horse and carriage carried on along the road, as Philip and the Ethiopian man talked and laughed and read and talked some more about the stories of Isaiah and Jesus and his friends, and stories from their own lives. What a lot to learn and share and understand!

At the end of the road they stopped by a river. 'What's to stop me being baptised right now?!' said the Ethiopian to Philip. He was so happy to have found a friend to help him understand what he had been reading. Now he understood who Jesus was, he wanted to do something to show how much he wanted to be Jesus' friend. So they climbed down from the carriage and jumped into the river. Philip splashed the water over the Ethiopian man to baptise him and they both shouted a big 'Thank you!' to God.

Jo Love, Spill the Beans

The charioteer's bar room tale
(Acts 8:26–39)

As if telling a tale in a bar a few weeks after arriving home.

An eventful journey? Indeed it was, though not in the way you might think. No attacks by highwaymen, no broken chariot wheels, only the usual ration of bed bugs and suspect food. But His Excellency reckons it changed his life.

You've noticed the effect on him, I imagine? Lightened up? Yes, that about describes it. Still very serious of course, and that's only proper for the keeper of the Queen's treasure, but he's found a smile I've never seen before.

How? Well, there's a tale, and it happened in the middle of nowhere.

You recall we'd been up north, to Jerusalem. Odd sort of city. No river to speak of. Been there for centuries. Not a patch on Meroe, our capital on the Nile. Romans everywhere, of course, but they allow the Jews to practise their religion, which is what His Excellency went for. Pilgrimage, he called it, though I can't see why he holds on to the tradition. A eunuch can't enter their temple or offer sacrifices. Jews would see it as an insult to their God: a man without all his bits, no matter how clever he is.

So His Excellency was in a low mood when we set off back to Ethiopia. Not helped by the scenery. The road south of Jerusalem's pretty bleak, and the chariot was lurching. He asked me to slow down so he could read a new scroll he'd bought, a posh copy of writing by one of the Jewish prophets. He was reading it aloud; asked me occasionally what I thought. Now my money's on Isis for divine favours, but I must say this chap Isaiah sounded very poetic, even though I didn't know the language.

Then, all of a sudden, I sense that the horses have heard something. I turn my head and there's a man running towards us from the Jerusalem direction. I'm ready to set the horses to a gallop. But he's respectably dressed, this stranger, and carrying no arms. Maybe he's a messenger. Perhaps the Queen has business for us to transact on the journey.

His Excellency has continued calmly reading. He trusts me to deal with the hazards on the road. I slow the horses to walking pace to allow the stranger to catch up, while making sure he sees I have my hand on my dagger. To my surprise, he does not greet His Excellency by any of his titles, but just blurts out: 'Do you understand what you are reading?!'

I am ready to strike the impertinent rascal down with my whip, but His Excellency not only signals me to halt, but invites the man to join him up on the chariot. The two of them sit talking as we travel for miles through the wilderness.

I only catch fragments. Something about Jesus: how he was a radical preacher that the Romans and the priests had conspired to execute in Jerusalem a while back. I'd heard strange tales about him in the stables. The stranger, a Greek-speaking Jew called

Philip, seems to link Jesus' story to references to lambs and sacrifices in the scroll. From the way His Excellency reacts, the message is that he can be included after all.

Just as I wonder how far this Philip intends to travel with us, we come to a river, or what passes for one in those dried-up parts. While I'm looking at how to ford it, His Excellency jumps down, tosses me his cloak, and he and Philip step out into a deep pool. To cut a long story short, he's becoming a follower of this Jesus, who he claims isn't so dead after all, and showing it through a dunking in the river, which the Jews call baptism.

I still don't know what to make of it. It makes no sense: and yet His Excellency has changed, found a wholeness, if you can say that of a eunuch. And there was some power at work in that desert spot. I could feel it, and I sensed the horses could too. And I'll tell you the strangest thing: that Philip just vanished, there at the river. I looked for him all around, for it's a lonely spot and a long way from anywhere. 'Don't worry,' says His Excellency. 'God's Spirit has moved him on.'

Kit Walkham

Ananias' prayers (Acts 9:1–19)

I had heard stories about this man they called Saul, who came from Tarsus.

He was in with all the Jewish leaders. They trusted him.

He stood there holding the coats of the members of the Council whilst they stoned Stephen.

He had a letter from the High Priest authorising him to arrest the followers of Jesus and bring them in chains to Jerusalem. He had even threatened to murder any Christians, or followers of the Way as he called them, that he found.

If people talked to me about Saul – I told them to keep clear of him. He was a dangerous man.

I'm a follower of Jesus, a Christian. I belong to the church in Damascus. Since Jesus died and came back to life it seems as if he's everywhere, in everything. When I pray I can feel Jesus close to me.

One day when I was praying, Jesus spoke to me. He said my name: 'Ananias.' He told me to go to Straight Street in the city, to the house of a man called Judas. He told me that I would find Saul of Tarsus there. He had been there blinded, and without food and drink for three days.

I told Jesus that I knew about this man, about all the trouble he had caused to the Christians in Jerusalem, about his authority from the High Priest to arrest any Christians that he found. And Jesus told me that Saul was praying, and that he had told Saul that a man called Ananias would come and lay hands on him, and he would be able to see again.

I really didn't want to go and find Saul. He could be pretending to be blind, and when I got there he might arrest me. But Jesus told me that Saul had been chosen to tell people about the Christian faith, chosen to talk with Jews and Gentiles.

So I went and found the house. I put my hands on Saul and I prayed. I called him brother and I told him that Jesus had sent me to pray for him. As I prayed, something like fish scales seemed to fall from his eyes and he could see again.

Then Saul got up and those of us in the house baptised him. Then we shared our food with Saul, and slowly, over a few days, he recovered his strength.

It's amazing how people can change. Saul of Tarsus, later he was called Paul, became a great preacher and teacher in the church. I was glad that Jesus had asked me to pray for him.

Ruth Burgess, Spill the Beans

Ananias' story

(Acts 9:1–19)

Hello.

I'm Ananias. I live in Damascus.

I'm a Christian. A follower of Jesus.

Something strange happened to me last week.

I was saying my prayers, and listening, and it seemed like Jesus was talking to me.

Jesus said my name: 'Ananias'. And I said, 'Yes, Jesus.'

Jesus gave me a job to do. He wanted me to go to the house of my friend Judas.

And he wanted me to talk to a man called Saul, who came from Tarsus.

When I heard the name Saul, I was worried.

I'd heard about this man. He was a rabbi.

An important one. He had arrested lots of Christians in Jerusalem. Now he was here.

I told Jesus what I thought. That talking to Saul was not a good idea. Saul was trouble for Christians.

I was scared. I didn't know if Saul was to be trusted. It might just be a trick to find out who the Christians were in Damascus.

Jesus listened. And then said to me, 'I know about Saul. I have talked to Saul. Saul has changed. He has become a Christian.'

Jesus then told me that Saul had been blinded by a bright light and that I was to go and pray with him, then he would be able to see again.

Jesus had told me what he wanted me to do, so I went.

Judas lives in Straight Street. Most people smile when I tell them that, but that's what it's called, 'Straight Street', and no, it's not got any bends or corners!

When I got to Judas' house, Judas came to the door – he looked scared too!

Saul was in the house. He looked dazed and Judas said that Saul had not been eating or drinking for three days.

I wasn't really sure what to do, but I took a deep breath and then I talked to Saul. I told Saul that the same Jesus who had talked to him on the road to Damascus had talked to me too.

I told Saul that I had been sent to pray with him, and I went over to him, put my hands on him and prayed that he might see. It was weird. Something like fish scales fell from Saul's eyes and he could see.

I didn't know what to do next, but Saul did. He gave us both a hug – and then said he was starving!

I was too, all this praying is hard work.

So Judas went and got some food and we had a feast. When you've shared food with someone it's hard to think of them as an enemy.

I think Saul might turn out to be OK!

John Murning, Spill the Beans

Will something happen to us?

(Acts 9:1–19)

In an upper room, surrounded by friends,
something happened to Thomas.

On a busy road, with other travellers,
something happened to Saul.

In this building among other Christians,
will something happen to us?

Spill the Beans

Spot the similarities

(Acts 9:36–43)

Voice 1: One writer.

Two stories.

Spot the similarities!

Spot the differences!

Let's go ...

Voice 2: In a house near the Lake of Galilee, a little girl was dying.

Voice 3: In a house in a town called Joppa, a woman had died.

Voice 2: Jairus, the little girl's father, asked Jesus to pray for his daughter.

Voice 3: The friends of the woman, who was called Tabitha, asked Peter to pray for her.

Voice 2: The little girl died. Jesus and his disciples arrived at Jairus' house.

Voice 3: Peter arrived at Tabitha's house.

Voice 2: Lots of people were at the house crying and mourning for Jairus' daughter.

Voice 3: Lots of people were at the house crying and mourning for Tabitha.

Voice 2: Jesus sent most of them away.

Voice 3: Peter sent them all away.

Voice 2: Jesus took Peter, James and John and the child's parents into her room.

Voice 3: Peter took no one into Tabitha's room.

Voice 2: Jesus took the little girl by the hand and told her to 'Get up'.

Voice 3: Peter took Tabitha by the hand and told her to 'Get up'.

Voice 2: The child got up at once.

Voice 3: Peter helped Tabitha to her feet.

Voice 2: Jesus told the girl's parents to get her something to eat.

Voice 3: Maybe Tabitha wasn't hungry …

Voice 2: Jesus told the girl's parents not to tell anyone what had happened.

Voice 3: Peter called Tabitha's friends and showed them that she was alive.

Voice 1: One writer. Two stories.

What was going on?

Both events happened?

Luke, the writer, had a reason for making the stories sound similar?

The stories got mixed up?

What do you think?

Ruth Burgess, Spill the Beans

Behind my story

(Acts 9:36–43)

This story reminds us of other stories in the Bible, such as Jairus' daughter and Elijah and Elisha. Here we take today's story and link it with these, and other, stories.

Have five people standing in a line in the central aisle of the church. The first voice is closest to the door. As people finish their last line, the next person in line picks up the story, so that the whole forms a 'chain reaction' of stories.

Voice 1: I am Tabitha.
I am a clothes maker,
a disciple of Jesus,
and resurrected one.
For I was dead,
but now I am alive.
I was on my bed surrounded
by mourning widows,
and Peter turned
and asked them to leave,
and he breathed life
into me again.
I am part of resurrection's story,
but behind my story …

Voice 2: … is my story.
I am Jairus' daughter,
small friend of Jesus,
and resurrected one.
I was dead but now I am alive,
for I was in my room,
surrounded by grieving family,
and Jesus arrived too late for me.
He turned and asked them
all to leave,
and breathed life into me,

and then we ate together.
I am part of resurrection's story,
but behind my story …

Voice 3: … is my story.
I am the son of a
Shunammite woman
who called on Elisha to help.
But I was already dead
in my room
with a few companion mourners
which he asked to leave.
Then he bent over me
and breathed life into me,
and my body grew warm again,
and I sneezed and breathed
once more.
I am part of resurrection's story,
but behind my story …

Voice 4: … is my story.
I am the son
of the widow of Zarephath.
Elijah the prophet,
having run away,
had been staying with us.
We were poor with only enough
oil and flour for a day's meal,
but they never ran out.
But I became ill,
and I died,
and Elijah stretched me out
on my bed,
and then stretched himself out,
and cried out to God,
and life returned to my body.
I am part of resurrection's story,
but behind my story …

Voice 5: ... is my story,
the story that always moves
towards life.
I am God,
and I am the story of resurrection.
But within my story,
is every story
of someone truly subversive,
who believes in their capacity
to transform lives.
Yet this is your story too,
living life
amongst all that
is slowly decaying.
You are part of
resurrection's story too.
Tell it again for me,
the story that always travels
towards life.

Roddy Hamilton, Spill the Beans

We can do it!

(Acts 13:1–3, 14:8–18)

Paul: Barnabas?

Barnabas: Yes, Paul.

Paul: Barnabas, what happened?

Barnabas: I'm not sure.

Paul: They thought we were gods!

Barnabas: They called me Zeus.

Paul: And they thought I was Hermes.

Barnabas: Their priest brought oxen and flowers. They were going to offer a sacrifice!

Paul: Oh, Barnabas, how could we get it so wrong?

Pause

Barnabas: Let's think about it, Paul; we don't want this to happen again; we need to learn from this. Let's go over what happened.

Paul: Well, when we got to Lystra I saw that man, sitting by the roadside – his legs were all withered – he looked as if he'd never walked. I could see that he was listening to me as I preached. I could see that he had the faith to be healed. So I said to him, 'Stand up', and he jumped up and began to walk and everyone went crazy – shouting out that we were gods who had come down to earth in human form.

Barnabas: Maybe that's where it started, Paul.

Paul: What do you mean?

Barnabas: Well, you healed that man before you finished explaining to them who Jesus was, and you didn't tell them that it was in the name of Jesus that the man was healed.

Paul: Barnabas, I didn't have a chance to. They were all shouting at once. No one would have heard me.

Barnabas: And they thought that the power of healing was in you, that you were a god.

Paul: You're right ... and I don't think us tearing our clothes helped.

Barnabas: Probably not – it's a Jewish custom – they wouldn't have understood it meant that we were really upset.

Paul: I did try to tell them that we were human beings, and that the living God made all of us, but they were too excited to listen.

Barnabas: And after that we had no chance of making ourselves understood.

Paul: Barnabas, we can't let this happen again.

Barnabas: We won't, Paul, we'll learn from our mistakes and maybe other people will learn from them too.

Paul: And we'll go on sharing the Good News about Jesus with everyone we meet – we have to ...

Barnabas: We will, Paul, we will.

Ruth Burgess, Spill the Beans

Sydney the chocolate Labrador
(Acts 13:1–3, 14:8–18)

Sometimes in trying to do the right thing, the good thing, we do not always realise the consequences, as was the case for Paul and Barnabas in Lystra. This story also talks about unintended consequences.

Clare was taking Sydney for a walk. Sydney was a brown Labrador who was five months old. Sydney could not quite pull Clare over but he was having a good try. They reached the zebra crossing and Clare told Sydney to sit down and he did.

When a car stopped, Clare told Sydney to stand up and they crossed the road safely. In the park Clare could let Sydney off the lead and she did. They had a great time. Sydney loved fetching his ball and Clare threw it for him lots of times.

Clare sat down for a few moments on a park bench. Sydney sat down at her feet. Clare got a chocolate biscuit out of her pocket. Sydney looked up at her with his big brown eyes. Clare began to eat her biscuit. Sydney kept on looking at her. Mum had said that Sydney should not be given any food between meals but he looked so hungry … and they had both been running around, and it was still an hour until dinnertime.

Clare looked at Sydney and Sydney looked at Clare and Clare broke a piece off her biscuit and gave it to Sydney. Well, mum had also said it was good to share things, and Sydney looked hungry, so she had shared her biscuit with Sydney. Sydney swallowed the piece of biscuit in one gulp and then he wagged his tail.

On the way home Sydney did as he was told and sat at the roadside before crossing the road. He did pull a bit on the lead, but only a little bit. Clare ate her dinner and then went round to play with her friend Mark for the afternoon. She got home in time for her tea.

Before Clare had her tea she usually took Sydney for a quick walk. 'Where's Sydney, mum?' Clare asked her mother. 'I'll walk him up and down the street.'

'He's in his basket,' said Clare's mum. 'He's been very quiet all afternoon.'

Clare went over to Sydney's basket. 'Oh, mum …

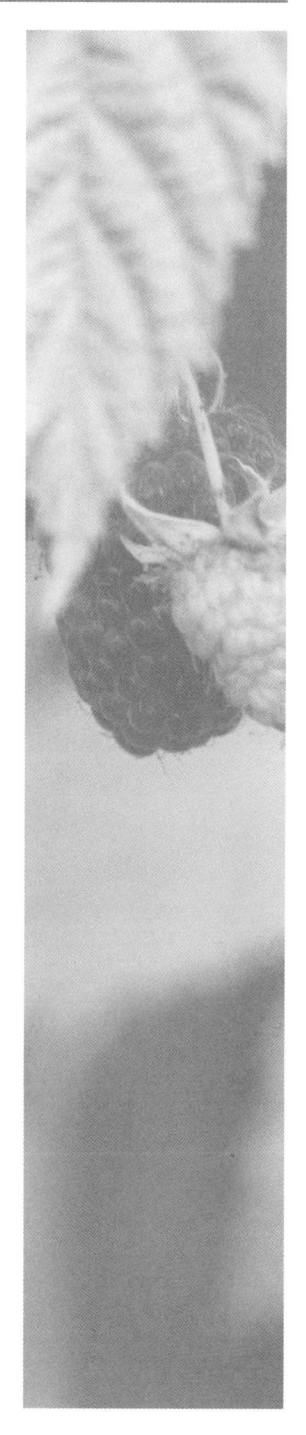

Look!' said Clare. 'Sydney has been sick.'

'He must have eaten something that didn't agree with him,' said Clare's mum. 'Go and get a mop and bucket, Clare, and we can clean the floor.'

As they cleaned the floor Sydney looked at Clare with his big brown eyes and Clare smiled.

Clare thought back to their morning in the park and then she remembered what she had given Sydney. She told mum about the park and the bench and the chocolate biscuit.

'Oh well,' said mum, 'you know now, and so does Sydney, dogs and chocolate biscuits are not a good idea. I don't think you'll make the same mistake again.'

Clare agreed.

And Sydney? He just looked at both of them and wagged his tail.

Ruth Burgess, Spill the Beans

Paul and Lydia
(Acts 16:9–15)

Paul and Lydia should read from separate places, each in effect doing a monologue, until they begin to react to each other from Paul's line ending 'she insisted'.

Paul: At last, a clear sign from the Lord. We were to go to Macedonia!

Lydia: At last, after a few days' trading, time to go home.

Paul: We sailed from Troas, spent a night on the island of Samothrace, then continued to Neapolis on the Macedonian coast, and from there a long walk inland to the town of Philippi.

Lydia: We sent a good load of purple cloth from Neapolis on the boat heading west to Troas, then returned to Philippi.

Paul: It was still a few days until the Sabbath, so we tried to keep busy, getting to know our way around, talking to the locals and looking out for likely places where worshippers might gather for prayer.

Lydia: I was eager for the Sabbath, as ever, but it was a busy few days. I noticed some new faces around town, some of them had accents not unlike the region of my old home, Thyatira. I wondered if they were traders of some kind.

Paul: One of our group met some textile traders. He heard talk that the most successful dealer in town is a woman, Lydia, from Thyatira – small world! She has a reputation for her spirituality too, although she's not Jewish.

Lydia: It seems the group of visitors are preachers and have travelled all over, from Pamphylia and Phrygia. Friends tell me the leader is quite a charmer. And celibate, part of his religious convictions apparently. They are Jews, but claim some new teaching after a rabbi from Nazareth.

Paul: When the Sabbath came, we made for the river. It seemed the most natural of meeting places.

Lydia: When the Sabbath came, we made for the river, where we always gathered.

Paul: It was easy to pick out the textiles queen … dressed in the stuff of her trade, and she hadn't completely lost her accent!

Lydia: The Nazarene's followers showed up for prayer. Easy to pick out the charmer. He does like the sound of his own voice!

Paul: We sang songs and shared the prayers of our traditions, teaching them the prayer the Lord taught us. Then they asked more about us, who we were, why we were there – and that was me – I was on a roll about Jesus!

Lydia: They all deferred to the charming Paul, as he's called, when we asked them about their faith. He just lit up the more he talked, but there was no boast about himself; it was all about this Jesus, the rabbi. Paul himself had tried to crush his following, until he had a dramatic encounter with Jesus after his death! He told us how it happened on the Damascus road ... my heart missed a beat! When I was a child, I travelled that road once with my father! Was my heavenly father now speaking to me through this preacher? I started clinging to his every word!

Paul: I got carried away describing what happened that day on the road to Damascus, and I suddenly caught the eye of the purple-cloth dealer; her gaze was fixed on me. I just prayed that God would give me the words for her.

Lydia: What a gift for preaching. He was extraordinary!

Paul: What a gift for listening. She was extraordinary!

Lydia: When he spoke of baptism, there was nothing I wanted more than to simply step into the river for that blessing, and the rest of my family followed.

Paul: What a glorious baptism, simple and spontaneous! She didn't care for a minute about ruining her dress! She waded in, and before we knew it, the rest of her household followed, praise God!

Lydia: It was obvious what to do next – we invited the whole band of Paul and his friends to come back to the house and stay with us a while. They didn't seem to be carrying much in the way of dry clothes anyway!

Paul: Next thing was, Lydia invited us all to stay at her house for a while. She said our clothes needed to be dried out for a start. We hesitated – but she insisted!

Lydia: I insisted!

Paul: And we talked late into the night.

Lydia: We talked about God working in ordinary ways ...

Paul: ... and God working in extraordinary ways

Lydia: ... to make things happen.

Paul: That day, I just did what I love, and talked!

Lydia: That day, I just did what I love, and listened!

Paul: What a generous and incredible woman.

Lydia: What a charmer! Though I'm not sure that purple is your colour.

Jo Love, Spill the Beans

Two very different people
(Acts 16:9–15)

Long ago, when people first started meeting together as church groups, they thought that maybe the things that were different about them would be a real problem.

Maybe it would mean they could not be friends. Maybe it would mean they could not be the church together.

I wonder what happened when two very different people met each other? One day, Paul met Lydia.

Paul was a man and Lydia was a woman. Could they be friends? Could they be the church together?

They came from different cities, and Lydia had moved to a different country too! Could they be friends? Could they be the church together?

What Paul was good at was making tents. What Lydia was good at was buying and selling expensive purple cloth. Could they be friends? Could they be the church together?

Paul probably didn't have a lot of money. Lydia had plenty of money; she was very rich. Could they be friends? Could they be the church together?

Paul had seen Jesus in a vision and knew a lot about him. Lydia didn't know anything about Jesus, but she loved God. Could they be friends? Could they be the church together?

Paul was a Jew. Lydia wasn't a Jew. Could they be friends? Could they be the church together?

Right from the beginning, when the church was new, God has asked people who are very different to be friends and to be the church together. Paul and Lydia did it! So can we.

Jo Love, Spill the Beans

The business woman
(Acts 16:11–15)

I took over the business when my husband died; we had no children and had always worked together, so it was natural that I should, in spite of what people said – that a woman couldn't run a business, it wasn't fitting or I didn't have the brains, or business men wouldn't deal with me! They should see the business now!

It was the business that eventually persuaded my father to let us marry when I fell in love with its owner; he specialised in purple cloth, and the purple dye was very expensive. It takes the shells from 250,000 molluscs to make one ounce of dye. So it only made sense to make high-quality cloths and garments, with a correspondingly high markup!

But the man I fell in love with was a proselyte, that is, a Gentile who believes in the Jewish faith, and my father thought it was all a load of nonsense and didn't want me to get mixed up with a foreign religion; we're Greeks by origin, though the family now lives in Thyatira.

I must admit, I was attracted by the rich lifestyle and the fine clothes my husband's family had, but I fell in love with his respect for others, his fair dealing with business associates, his care for his employees, his generosity and his relationship with the God I came to know through him.

So my father gave in, and when he saw how happy we were he was glad he had.

It was a devastating blow to us all when my husband died suddenly, and my family wanted me to go back to them, but I knew I had to carry on with the business and needed to stay with the other believers in the Jewish God – they were my friends and they helped me through the bad times, helped me come closer to the God we shared; that was partly why I moved to Philippi, though there were good business reasons as well.

We didn't have a building to meet in, so we gathered on the Sabbath down by the river.

One Sabbath a man called Paul and his friends appeared, and spoke to us about Jesus.

I was so glad to meet him and to listen to him – his words made so much sense and completed the faith which I had come to believe in. It didn't take me long to know that I wanted to join this group of Christians; and along with several others – amid much joy and celebration – I was baptised in the river by our worship place!

It only made sense after that to invite Paul and his companions to stay at my house – I had plenty of room and servants to care for us.

Paul and I even discussed the possibility of making tents out of purple canvas!

Helen Barrett

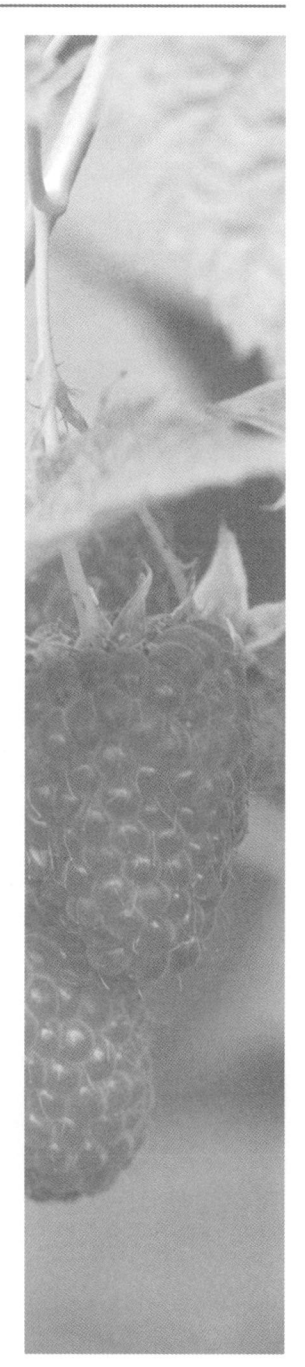

An old wife's tale

(Acts 16:16–40)

A dialogue between the wife of the jailer and her friend, recounting the strange events in their town.

Jenny: Is it true, Beth? You're the talk of the town for taking in a pair of escaped prisoners last night. Is it true?

Beth: They saved my man's life, Jenny.

Jenny: Saved his life? Did the other inmates set on him? What happened?

Beth: Well, you felt the tremors like everyone else. It brought half the prison down. They could have all made a run for it.

Jenny: Surely some of them did?

Beth: That's what Danny thought when he woke up to the walls caving in. He was ready to run himself through.

Jenny: So what happened? You're not going to tell me they didn't scarper when they had the chance?

Beth: If they'd got away, Danny's life wouldn't have been worth living. He'd have been done for, earth tremors or not; he would have been blamed. Dereliction of duty. By the grace of God, that man Paul saved him.

Jenny: Paul? Who's Paul? And what did he do?

Beth: I washed his wounds and cooked him a dinner and let him and his friend Silas rest in our home last night.

Jenny: Aye, so I've heard! But why? What makes a criminal your sudden hero?

Beth: Paul saw Danny draw his sword … and knew what he was about to do, and he stopped him, Jenny, he just yelled out: 'Don't do it! We're all here!' Danny can hardly remember a thing but he remembers that piercing shout, cutting right through the chaos; he says it was like hearing the voice of an angel, and he just froze, and they came running and pulled his sword out of his hand.

Jenny: Were they not thinking of killing him themselves! Why wouldn't they? Their jailer, and now they're all on the loose …

Beth: I know, I know. But they didn't. Not one of them harmed him, or each other.

Pause

Beth: Danny says they were all singing before the tremors started.

Jenny: Singing? In the jail?

Beth: I know. Sounds crazy. It was Paul and his companion who started it. Danny put them in the stocks and they just started singing. Angels, I tell you …

Jenny: But weren't they the two accused of causing a disturbance in the city? They don't sound like angels to me. What were they up to, to get thrown in jail in the first place?

Beth: Do you know the wee girl who tells fortunes?

Jenny: Leila. Of course I do. What's she got to do with it? She's lost the power to do it any more.

Beth: That's right. Paul took her power away. Danny heard he just called on the name of Jesus, the Rabbi he says came back from the dead. Straight away, no more fortune-telling for Leila. Which took away the fortunes of her owners. So they stirred up no end of charges against Paul, and it all ended with a brutal flogging for him and his pal, and Danny being told to lock them up.

Jenny: Goodness me, what an over-reaction. Did you hear the upshot about Leila though? She's back home with her mother.

Beth: Oh, that's wonderful! What about all the money she owed?

Jenny: The guys who bought her don't care. Leila's no use to them now and she'd made them more money than any debts. She should have been home months ago. I bet her mother feels like she's got her child back from the dead!

Beth: And I've got my Danny ... back from the dead ...

Jenny: So what about your, erm, visitors?

Beth: They're recovering. We all are. They've been telling us all about their Jesus. We all got baptised!

Jenny: What did you do that for?!

Beth: Come and see, Jenny, come on and meet my guests ...

Jo Love, Spill the Beans

Jeb the jailer
(Acts 16:16–40)

Hello, I am Jeb the jailer. Yes, that is my job: to lock up people who have broken the law, and make sure none of them escapes. That is the important bit! Nobody escapes until the day they are allowed to go free again. If I let anyone escape, I would be in so much trouble for not doing my job properly.

But there was one night last week when I thought that every prisoner I had locked up was going to escape all at once. It was terrible! But it turned out fine. Let me tell you what happened.

The day before, two men were accused of causing unrest in my town. It was a strange case. They had not really done anything wrong. But they were punished terribly with whipping and beating, and I was ordered to put them in the most secure prison cell. I did what I was told and I even made them sit with their feet in the stocks. So there was no way they were moving at all. The funny thing was, they seemed to be okay with it. They were even quite nice and polite to me, asking me my name and telling me theirs. Paul and Silas. Nice chaps. What were they doing in my jail?

When they had settled down, they started singing. Singing! I had never had any singing prisoners before. Most of the other guys started singing along with them too. The songs were all about God. They were beautiful songs! Well, it was going to be the most peaceful night in prison I had even known. Everyone singing and two men in the secure cell who were not going to be any trouble at all.

'There's no way they will be thinking of escaping!' That is what I thought as I decided to sleep for a while at the prison gate. The sound of their singing sent me off to the land of dreams …

Later on, in the middle of the night, I was woken up by rumbling noises and shouts of fear. What?! An earthquake perhaps? The ground was shaking, and pieces of rock and stone from the walls started falling down! The prison gate heaved and moved beside me and suddenly burst open! Oh my goodness, if the gate was open then maybe the stocks would be broken too. I could hear the noise of chains clashing. 'Oh no, all the prisoners are breaking out! They'll come running out of here any minute. I might as well kill myself!'

I reached for my sword, ready to die, because I couldn't live with letting my boss down and not doing my job properly. I am Jeb the jailer – I cannot let anyone escape, I just cannot!

My sword was in my hand, when I heard someone yelling in the darkness and footsteps running towards me, 'Jeb! Stop! Don't hurt yourself!' It was Paul! 'We're all here,' he cried, 'we're all here!'

I nearly fainted in shock as he reached me and pulled the sword out of my hand. But I pulled myself up, lit a lantern and saw for myself that he was telling the truth. Not one of the men in the cells had tried to run away. And my life had been saved. Jailer Jeb saved by prisoner Paul.

I took Paul and Silas back to my house. I knew by now they were good men, and we talked for ages about God, and sang some of the songs they had been singing through the night. They told me about Jesus, and I decided I wanted to follow Jesus and learn to live the way he had lived. Then Paul baptised me and my family, as a sign that we belong to God.

After our scary night, it was such a happy day. We had quite a party!

Jo Love, **Spill the Beans**

Who am I with?

(Acts 18:1–4)

Who do I belong to in this church of ours? Who gets my allegiance? Who am I with? Well, let me think …

I'm with Paul. Great guy! He baptised a few of us. But his real gift to us has been his preaching. Not that he's a polished performer. He's persuasive, though, and persistent. But not always polite! In fact, he can get pretty argumentative. I don't know where he gets his energy – he can go on debating for hours! Yep, that's Paul.

And I'm with Apollos. Great guy! Now Apollos, he's much more your skilled speaker. He was taught well by our Priscilla and Aquila. When we first knew him, the only baptism he knew about was from the practice of John the Baptist and his fiery message of the need to change our ways before the Messiah came. Paul put it well when he said that he planted the seeds among us and Apollos watered them. That's the kind of teamwork we've really benefitted from.

Then there's Peter. Great guy! I'm with Peter all the way. Where would we be without him? The Rock and then some! Travelling and teaching, being challenged and changed, embracing the Gentiles, enlarging his vision and thinking as he grasped the wide sweep of God's love for all.

But most of all, above all, beyond all, I'm with Jesus. Paul and Apollos and Peter never stop bringing us back to Jesus. In whose name are we baptised. Who gave up his life rather than give up his integrity. Who lives again, as real to us in spirit as he was to Peter in flesh.

Paul. Apollos. Peter. Christ. They get my allegiance. I belong to them. They're the ones I'm with. I thank God for them. One body. Many parts.

Jo Love, Spill the Beans

The best teacher?

(Acts 18:1–4)

One day after school, four children from the same class were walking home together. Katy, Tolu, Rachel and Kevin were talking about four of their visiting teachers.

On a Monday, Miss White came before lunch to do their drama lesson. Katy thought Miss White looked like an actor in her colourful clothes and with her ability to speak convincingly in lots of different accents!

On a Tuesday, Mrs Jamieson came to take gym time, which was sometimes in the gym hall, sometimes outside in the playground and occasionally meant a trip to the swimming pool. Tolu loved the way Mrs Jamieson was so enthusiastic about keeping fit and healthy. She had so much energy and never seemed to get tired with all the running around and exercise.

On Thursday afternoons, Mr Kelly came with his keyboard or his guitar and usually some percussion and always some great new songs for the class to do their music. Rachel had learned so much from Mr Kelly about how to play the guitar herself.

On Fridays after lunch, Mrs Galbraith came to teach art. Kevin used to hate art but now he quite liked it because Mrs Galbraith always said it was great to try out lots of ideas and keep experimenting, without worrying if things turned out looking perfect or not.

'Who do you think is the best one of our four visiting teachers?' asked Katy.

'The best one of all? Let me think …' wondered Tolu.

'That's hard to decide …' said Rachel.

Kevin screwed up his face, thinking about Miss White and Mrs Jamieson and Mr Kelly and Mrs Galbraith. Who was the best? Finally he asked Katy, 'Well, what do you think? You asked the question, Katy. So who do you think is the best?'

'Well, if what mattered most was colourful clothes and interesting voices, it would be …'

'Miss White!' the other three laughed.

'And if what mattered most was keeping us fit and healthy, it would be …'

'Mrs Jamieson!' the other three laughed.

'And if what mattered most was singing and keeping the beat, it would be …'

'Mr Kelly!' the other three laughed.

'And if what mattered most was experimenting and learning to make mistakes and not give up, it would be …'

'Mrs Galbraith!' the other three laughed.

'But I think that what matters most is being a great person and a great teacher, so the best is …'

'All of them!' joined in Tolu and Rachel and Kevin as they all giggled and felt glad.

'Isn't it brilliant?' said Katy. 'Not just one best teacher – but four! We're so lucky!'

You could ask the children what good but different qualities they see in some of their class teachers and visiting teachers.

Jo Love, Spill the Beans

Post-Easter lectionary passages

The widow of Zarephath
(1 Kings 17:1–24)

I often wondered why Elijah came to me.
He was a man of God, his God, the God of Israel, not mine.
I live in Zarephath, a town ruled by Sidon.

I was getting desperate.
The rains had not come for three years and there was a famine.
My supplies of flour and oil were practically exhausted.
Enough for one last meal before my son and I died of starvation.

And suddenly I was expected to house and feed Elijah.
I had been gathering sticks for a fire to bake what little food I had left.
And he asked me for water and bread.
I knew that I was obliged to provide them.
But I told him of our plight.
His reply was that God said that my supply of flour and oil would not fail
until the rains came.

Did he expect me to believe him?
But I did. He seemed to speak with authority.
Anyway, what had I to lose? We were about to die anyway.

I baked him some bread
and there was enough for my son and me as well.
He stayed with us for many days.
There was a space in the roof area where he slept.
And every day when I went to make bread, there was enough for that day.

What sort of man was this?
What sort of God did he believe in?

But then my son became ill.
And he stopped breathing.
And I wondered about this man of God.
Had he come to reveal my sins to God and was this my punishment?
Was my son dead because of him?

When he said, 'Give me your son', I was afraid.
What was he going to do?
He took him upstairs to his room.
I don't know what he did.
But after a while he brought him down alive and gave him to me.
'See, your son is alive,' he said.

I could see that.
What joy filled my heart!
To have my son restored to life again.

I looked at this man in a new light.
Now I really understood that he was a man of God.
A God who had great power.
A God, who through the word of Elijah,
could provide food in famine,
bring life back to a dead child
and bring the needed rain.

Yes, not long after he left us, the rain came.
The famine was over.
My son and I could live again.

Margaret Roe

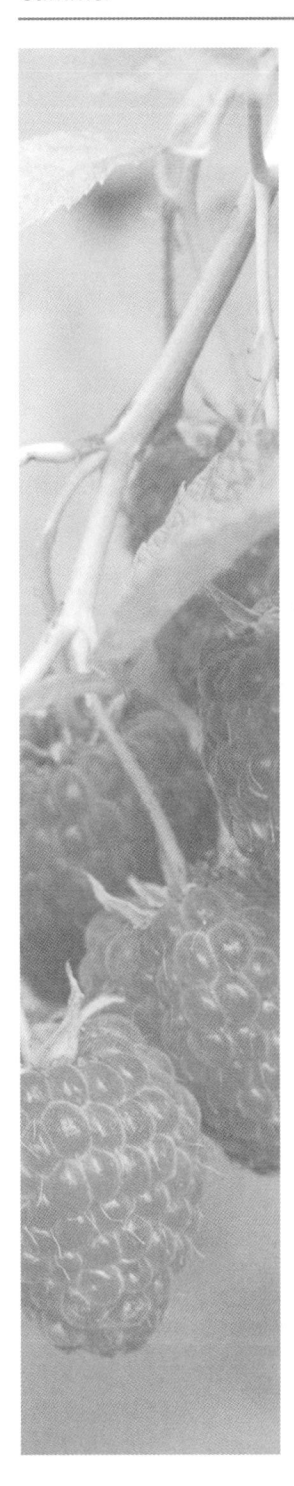

He's raving mad

(John 10:1–10)

To follow the reading. An unnamed Pharisee has a sarcastic, sneering rant about Jesus. Best delivered with no holds barred!

Monologue could be followed by one or two discussion questions, such as: What point do you think Jesus was making with the metaphors of the shepherd and gate? How have you experienced Jesus as a gateway to life?

He's raving mad! Well – did you hear him?

Don't listen to another word! Oh, but he's clever, I'll give him that. Using the language of the street to undermine respect for the authorities. Look at them all, hanging on his every word, traipsing round after him everywhere he goes, cheering him on when, yet again, he goes stirring things up in the synagogue.

Sheep and bandits, shepherds and voices, gates and gatekeepers … what is he getting at this time? I'll tell you who the gatekeepers are – we are! And you're right: we will not open the way to the likes of him, especially not after this latest near riot. This supposed curing of a common sinner who's been blind all his life and then comes parading his 'miraculous' sight and mocking us for demanding to know what that madman did to him.

'The sheep will not follow a stranger' … but they do, the common fools, they do! They follow him and lap up his dangerous talk. His voice is like a magnet to them. Sucking them in and filling their heads with the same nonsense that pours out of him.

'All who came before me are thieves and bandits, but

the sheep did not listen' ... Ah, but they did, oh so many times, brainwashed and led astray by umpteen false prophets declaring the latest fad for the good life. Which, of course, is exactly what he thinks he's offering himself.

'Life in all its fullness'... Oh really? 'Life in all its abundance' ... Well, that's some claim. No delusions of grandeur there; no, none at all.

Why are they so enchanted by him? He has the audacity to call us blind, but look at the way he dazzles and hooks them.

What do they see in him? What do they hear? It sounds like riddles, but some say he's crystal clear.

Life? Fullness of life? The gateway to life? Somehow I just don't see it.

Jo Love, Spill the Beans

Shuggie the shepherd
(John 10:1–10)

This is a story about Shuggie the shepherd. We're going to act out the way that Shuggie looked after his sheep. So first we need to build a sheep pen like the ones on the hills where Shuggie worked.

Guide a few children to sit in a small circle and hold hands, with one 'opening' in the circle where two of them don't join hands.

When the sheep needed to be kept safe from wolves, or needed shelter at night-time or in bad weather, Shuggie led them into the pen.

Pick someone to be Shuggie, with others as the sheep, and have Shuggie go into the circle through the opening, with sheep following.

When it was daytime and the weather was good, Shuggie led the sheep out of the pen to find grass and leaves to eat.

Shuggie goes out of the circle, sheep follow, and mime eating grass.

But there was one problem. How could Shuggie make the sheep stay in the pen if he fell asleep?

Take any suggestions and consider them.

Well, Shuggie turned himself into a gate! Yep, he lay down across the opening in the wall of the sheep pen!

Shuggie leads the sheep back inside the circle, then lies down across the gap, being the 'gate'.

What if a wolf tried to creep in? I think Shuggie would hear or feel the wolf, and jump up and chase it away!

Have someone be the wolf and try to step over a 'sleeping' Shuggie!

You could extend the story with a simple game where the children run around the room until you call out an action/scene: 'Build the sheep pen!' 'Night-time!' 'Sunny morning!' 'Rainy day!' 'Grass to munch!' 'Night-time!' 'Wolf is coming!' 'Wake up, Shuggie!' ... and so on.

Jo Love, Spill the Beans

I've read these verses at funerals
(John 14:1–14)

I've read these verses at funerals – they can be comforting.
They speak of a love that cares and prepares a place for us.
Perhaps a welcome to the banqueting table
with our name written on the place setting?
Maybe a room with a monogrammed towel folded on the bed?
Or an angelic announcement of our arrival to the gathering?

Yet somehow, deep down, that wouldn't comfort my troubled heart.
It wouldn't settle my anxiety, or still my fears.
You see, I've lived in places where I was known – but did not feel at home.
I have eaten at tables where words were hard to swallow
and left a bitter taste behind.
But there is comfort here in these words, Lord; we can feel it.
Your disciples felt it too – you wanted them to.
You were going to a place – certainly,

but you were longing most for your Father,
for the welcome-home embrace that takes the pain of the world away.

You were making a way home to the Father's heart,
to that eternal embrace that finally stills our fears and fulfils our longings.
And on arrival, you left the door wide open –
'Welcome home, child – to the place I have prepared for you.'

Paul Fillery

The house of many rooms
(John 14:1–7)

It said in scripture that it was a mansion with many rooms! There is no description about where it is, what it looks like, how it is made, and for how long the tenancy might be. There is no mention of the colour scheme or the style. I mean, will it be like a baronial castle, with musty smells and poor sanitation, or will it be clean and modern with the best of everything? Will each room be designed differently, according to our own tastes? Will it have a swimming pool, a large snooker table, a gigantic television and room service? Will someone make the beds and tidy up after us each day? Will it be like an old folks' home, or a godly squat?

And in this house, who will be my neighbours? Will I know them, recognise them, like them? Will they know who I am and what I did in the past? Will this house be a house of communal living, where we all have different responsibilities to the house, or will we be treated like kings and queens and waited on hand and foot?

What do I have to do to qualify for residence? Go to church, care for the poor, be a fighter of justice, a follower of Jesus? How is this measured? Is there a points system? Does God just build new rooms as and when they are needed?

O Jesus, am I misunderstanding your heavenly mansion? Is it just a place we all call home? A place where we can feel secure, safe and loved? A place where there is no conflict or bitterness or hatred? A place where all are welcomed regardless of their race, gender, colour or brand of religion? A place where hope is kindled, light and truth is revealed, compassion is practised and experienced? A place where God is truly present and sickness and death are banished?

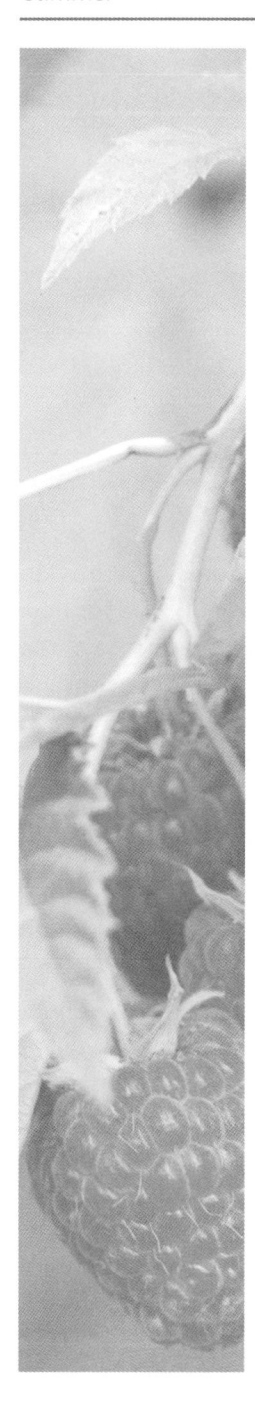

And in this heavenly mansion, God, will all our questions be answered? All our doubts be cast out? All our fears, worries and woes be banished forever? And if they are, then the house itself does not matter, because you are there and your Kingdom has come and you have been made known.

John Murning, Spill the Beans

A letter home
(John 17:1–26)

Hi Dad,
yes, it's me again;
yes, I wanted to talk to you again.
Here I am, your Son.
Your Chosen One.

And it's time.

Yes, the time has come,
and now your Son is going to do
what needs to be done.

And you will be known.
And you will be honoured.
And you will receive glory.
Because your Son is going to do it all ...
under your authority,
through your power,
and they will know at last
that it is you who sent the Son.
You who sent me.

I've done it all, Dad.
I ran the race and finished the task.

And these guys here,
these friends of mine –
the ones you gave me –
my special, special friends,
I've kept them with me,
shown them and taught them
and told them again
and shown them again.
Although they heard,
it took them time to fully grasp,
to fully know, and now they know –
you are the One!

Dad! Dad, please bless them;
help them to know and to trust
and to believe.

They are my guys,
but they are your guys too,
every one of them.
And they need you;
they need me;
they need us.

Love them, bless them,
help them, show them,
protect them
and, when the time comes,
bring them to glory, with us,
and make us one.

I love you, Dad, and I love my guys.

Your Son.

Julie Rennick, Spill the Beans

Rogationtide

Rogationtide

I first learned of Rogation Days while working on an exegesis of Leviticus 25 for a sermon I was giving in the rural church where I served. The more I read – the more excited I became. I knew the farmers in the congregation would be pleased too, to hear about honouring the land and the work they do. I also thought this was the answer for saving our planet Earth, and us, from ourselves. Pollution, global warming, climate change and all the damage humans have inflicted on the earth. The answer was simple – stop and rest!

Since that first sermon on Rogation Days, I have developed a new respect for the idea of Sabbath, not only for the earth, but for all that lives and depends on the earth. I now believe Sabbath rest is essential for the land and for our spiritual lives. It is key to growing closer to God. If each of us spent time in retreat every year, every month, if we took time each week, each day to pause and step away, the world would be a different place indeed. We know fields need to rest between planting seasons, and we need to rest from our ever-increasing exploitation of the earth's resources. Sabbath offers us time to step away and reflect on our lives, to find more innovative ways to preserve and share our resources, to restore and recycle what we have, and to become stewards of the gifts we have been given – the earth and all its wonders!

Indigenous people understand our human connection to the earth. In his 1854 lament, Chief Seattle of the Pacific Northwest expressed what he felt and saw was happening to the land, and said: *'This we know, the earth does not belong to us, we belong to the earth.'*

Rogation is a word left over from the days when local farmers were central to a particular community's survival and children grew up understanding the earth's cycles and knowing how food and animals grow, and that human health is dependent on the earth's health. Even though many rural churches are still surrounded by fields, Rogation Days are seldom celebrated. Special prayers for thanking God for the fruits of the earth fall under Thanksgiving or Harvest celebrations. Rogation Day has been buried beneath Earth Day and other days of conservation, which *do* help to open our eyes, but plough over the central purpose – our need for Sabbath rest.

Rebeka Maples

A prayer for Rogation Sabbath

O Rogation Sabbath,
welcome us into your silence:
no requirements, no expectations,
only heart meeting heart.

O Sabbath rest,
we take your forgiveness and hope
and lay down our burdens.
We seek your silence,
and when we find it
help us to linger there with you.

O Sabbath peace,
as silence sinks into our souls,
help us to pause in your serenity,
feel the comfort of your presence,
rest a while in your peace.

O Rogation Sabbath,
go with us now where we go;
though the world will take you from us,
bring us here again,
into a place of Sabbath rest.

Rebeka Maples

I have seen how light falls

(Theme: Summer light)

I have seen how light falls.
It circles in the wind
and scatters on the water.
It disappears when night comes
and returns when morning breaks.

When light falls at sunset
the colours fade from the sky
and soak into the earth.

When light falls
it kisses the trees and coats the hills
with grace from beyond the veil.

When light falls
all creation laments
and bows before its passing.

When light falls on the desert sand
it dances across the dunes
and chases each shooting star.

I have seen how light falls,
filtering through the space between,
shadowing what we have lost.

Rebeka Maples

Earth's wisdom

(Theme: Awareness of the earth)

She gave us all she could;
it was enough from where she stood
but not enough to feed our greed.

Earth's wisdom could not hold;
there was nothing left when all was sold;
beauty and grace
abandoned at bargain prices,
now they stand
monuments to highrises.

She sent messengers with
warnings of destruction;
drowned by other sounds
her words were ridiculed and denied;
science was her guide
and love her navigator;
she cries now,
only empty platitudes to liberate her.

Rebeka Maples

A new season comes

(Theme: Changing of the seasons)

Summer ends.
Flowers fade.
Birds flock together.
Nature's green is turning.
Summer moves into autumn.

Life fades.
Shadows announce the end.
Beauty appears in rising moons and setting suns.
Flowers bloom, before their descent into winter's rest,
sheltered from the cold, to rise again,
bringing new colour, soaring to new heights.
What treasures will they offer when a new season comes?

Summer fades.
A new season comes, bringing new demands.

Another way of living.
One season moves into another, yet it is not the end
for hope rises again and again
with each falling leaf, each fading flower,
each bird that migrates to a warmer place,
each face that marks the passing of another year.
It is not the end.
A new season comes.

Rebeka Maples

Walking the fields

(Theme: Summer heat and drought)

Walking round the field,
crunch, crunch, crunch.

Stepping on dried-out grass
dying from summer's heat
and the farmer's deadly spray,
crunch, crunch, crunch.

Walking past neatly planted furrows,
roots rising higher, digging deeper,
in the scorching sun,
stepping on remnants of last year's growth,
crunch, crunch, crunch.

Past rows and rows of eager stalks
reaching high into the sky
seeking sun and praying for rain,
leaves growing thinner
desperate for a drink.
Walking round the field,
crunch, crunch, crunch.

Path of dying grass
flattened between dormant fields
planted after spring floods.
Farmers waiting anxiously
unsure of weather and yield,
waiting, knowing nothing they do
will make the rains come.
Sun high in the noonday sky
drying out dried-out fields,
crunch, crunch, crunch.

Earth cracking into deeper crevices
waiting, yearning for summer showers
to fill dried-out creek beds
for basking frogs, passing geese and lone herons,
waiting for the rains
to wash away stagnant residue
and quench dying life,
crunch, crunch, crunch.

Rebeka Maples

An elemental Rogation liturgy

Introduction

These prayers can be used in rural or urban areas and although they are full of suggestions, the local environment must be your starting point when planning a route. The basic concept is to walk around the parish/the local area, praying for all who work there. In rural areas it may be possible to pray for growing crops. In urban areas it might make more sense to pray outside a local food shop or in a park. There may be particular factories or landmarks that you want to include.

There are four liturgies, based on the elements (water, air, fire, earth), and they can be used in any order. There are suggestions for a closing order of worship, and also for prayers for those who are not in paid work. When there are children involved in the worship a stop near a local school could be included.

The four liturgies follow a format:

- *Suggestions for a meeting place*
- *Opening responses*
- *Psalm (verses from Psalm 104)*
- *Prayers*
- *Action*

There are some suggestions for songs and hymns. An accompanying band might be useful in moving from place to place. You might also want to create an elemental banner/s.

When choosing actions choose ones that are within your resources and fit in with your timing. These prayers could take all day, or an afternoon, or could be used as separate acts of worship on different days.

Local industries and environment will focus which workers you pray for and you might choose to create a responsive prayer to enable the whole group to make a verbal response. The last suggestion for prayers in each section is based on a global justice issue … there may be other situations you have concerns about.

Try to make your route accessible for differently-abled people and/or plan stopping-places that can be accessed by transport. The liturgies are designed to be led by a number of leaders. If you meet in an unsheltered spot you might need to think about audibility, especially when children are reading.

Each act of worship is complete in itself and any order can be used, depending on the local environment. You could finish at any of the four meeting places or you could have a closing act of worship somewhere else.

These prayers have also been used within a church building, using symbols to focus on each element (e.g. candles, blown bubbles, food, water poured from a jug into a bowl) and including movement within the building.

These prayers deliberately include elements of fun. Enjoy yourselves!

Musical resources

Many traditional songs and hymns have elemental themes, and if worship is outdoors it is probably best to stick with what is familiar.

Using chants rather than hymns will eliminate the need for song sheets. The use of songs with choruses with which everyone can join in has the same advantage. Many traditional work songs are of this type.

The following songs can all be found in the *Church Hymnary*, 4th edition:

- 'All creatures of our God and King'
- 'All things bright and beautiful'
- 'I love the sea'
- 'May the God of peace go with us'
- 'Oh the life of the world'
- 'She sits like a bird'
- 'The peace of the earth be with you'
- 'Touch the earth gently'
- 'We are marching in the light of God'
- 'Who put the colours in the rainbow'
- 'You shall go out with joy'

Music (use of a drum?) and songs may be played or sung within the liturgies and when moving between meeting places.

FIRE

Meeting place: under a streetlight, near a solar light, round a bonfire, near a restaurant, by a barbecue, round a brazier, in bright sunlight …

Burning in a bush
blazing in a fiery pillar
Moses met you
Come God and meet us now

Roasting fish in embers
sitting round a bonfire
disciples met you
Come God and meet us now

Fire around their heads
holiness in their lives
believers met you
Come God and meet us now

Ps 104

Praise God, O my soul.
O God, my God, how great you are.
You are covered with majesty and glory;
you cover yourself with light;
you use the winds as your messengers
and flashes of lightning as your servants.
You created the moon to mark the months;
the sun knows the time to set.
You look at the earth and it trembles,
you touch the mountains and they pour out smoke.

Alternative/additional readings:

Acts 2:1–4
Exodus 3:1–5
Daniel 3

Pray for: electricians, chefs, welders, cooks, streetlamp servicers and menders, firework producers, workers on oil rigs, firefighters, candle-makers, solar panel fitters, scientists, metal workers, crematorium workers, lighters of birthday candles, those without warmth and shelter …

Action: light lamps, light torches, cook food, set off fireworks, make a bonfire, light sparklers, install a solar lamp …

AIR

Meeting place: on a hilltop, airfield, playground, near a roundabout or swings, near a wind-tunnel (e.g. between two blocks of flats), on high ground …

Star-maker God
wind blower
rain bringer
Breath of God, breathe on us now

Storyteller God
bird watcher
hill climber
Breath of God, breathe on us now

Pentecostal God
fire dancer
life bringer
Breath of God, breathe on us now

Ps 104

Praise God, O my soul.
O God, my God, how great you are.
You have spread out the heavens like a tent
and built your home in the heights.
You use the clouds as your chariot
and ride on the wings of the wind.
The cedars of Lebanon get plenty of rain there,
the birds build their nests.
When you send out your Spirit all life is created.
You breathe new life into the earth.

Alternative/additional readings:

Job 37:5–12
Ezekiel 37:1–10
John 3:5–9

Pray for: astronauts, tyre-makers, wind turbine makers, aeroplane crews, helicopter pilots and rescue crews, hang-gliders, fairground workers, beekeepers, steeplejacks, falconers, those who live in air-polluted environments …

Action: fly kites, blow bubbles, have a turn on a roundabout or a swing, give each other a swing (gently), climb a tower, play on a bouncy castle/trampoline, jump up and down, fly a flag or a banner …

EARTH

Meeting place: garden, allotment, park, graveyard, near a food shop, by grass or weeds growing through concrete, on a hill, on a footpath, in a quarry, near a building site …

You, God, are our rock
our sure foundation
our solid ground
You are our strength

You, Jesus, are our bread
our death and resurrection
our common ground
You are our hope

You, Holy Spirit, are our wildness
our loving wisdom
our holy ground
You are our joy

Ps 104

Praise God, O my soul.
O God, my God, how great you are.
You have set the earth firmly on its foundations
and it will never be moved.
You make grass for the cattle
and plants for us to use
so that we can grow our crops
and produce wine to make us happy,
olive oil to make us cheerful
and bread to give us strength.

Alternative/additional readings:

Psalm 96:10–13
Matthew 13:1–9
John 12:20–26

Pray for: town-planners, builders, farmers, archaeologists, shopkeepers, gardeners, JCB drivers, mountain rescue teams, tunnellers and quarry workers, park-keepers, gravediggers, walkers, miners, those who are hungry …

Action: buy food, eat food, plant seeds, pick fruit or vegetables, build a cairn of stones, make sandcastles, dig a hole (and fill it up afterwards!) …

WATER

Meeting place: fountain, sewer cover, drain, tap, near a river, near the sea, swimming pool, pond, near a brewery, a distillery or bottled water factory, near a water mill, on a bridge over a stream, at a well, near puddles …

Playful God
creator of sea monsters
keeper of the shorelines
We praise you

Joyful God
listener at a well
healer by a pool
We praise you

Mysterious God
dancer at creation
mover over the deep dark waters
We praise you

Ps 104

Praise God, O my soul.
O God, my God, how great you are.
When you rebuked the waters they fled.
They rushed away when they heard your shout of command.
They flowed over the mountains and into the valleys
to the place you had made for them.
You set a boundary they can never pass
to keep them from covering the earth again.
The ocean is large and wide.
The ships sail on it, and in it plays Leviathan,
the sea monster you made to amuse you.

Alternative/additional readings:

Jonah 1:17–2:10
Mark 4:35–41
John 5:1–8

Pray for: plumbers, engineers, vine growers, swimming baths attendants, sewerage workers, fishers, winemakers, brewery workers, distillers, umbrella-makers, water bailiffs, lifeboat crews, factory workers, those who have no access to fresh clean water …

Action: sprinkle each other with water, drink a local beverage, paddle in a local pond, play Pooh sticks at a bridge, sail a model boat, stamp in puddles, wash one another's hands and/or feet …

UNEMPLOYMENT

Although the focus of rogation prayers is on people who are working, the reality of most locations is that there will be people who are not able to find work.

These two prayers are for those who are unemployed:

Remind me
in the days
when there is no paid work

in the days
when no one is willing to hire me

in the days
when the system wears me down

remind me, God,
you love me
and need me.

Day in, day out
no money
no meaning.

Day in, day out
no security
no strength.

Day in, day out
no work
no warmth.

Day in, day out
God breathes
God listens.

Day in, day out
God loves
God loves me.

It may also be good to include space in your prayers for those who are ill and for those whose caring responsibilities prevent them from taking paid work. Also for those who are prevented from working by disabling working environments.

CLOSING ACT OF WORSHIP AND CELEBRATION

If possible finish with a celebratory act that includes all four elements:

- Food, drink, bouncy castle and fireworks
- Picnic, barbecue, Pooh sticks and kite-flying
- A meal with candles, balloons and a local beverage
- Paddling, sandcastle-building, kites and sunbathing
- Puddle-splashing followed by a visit to the fairground and chips

Opening responses

For warm sunlight
bonfires
and blazing stars
We thank you

For clean air
birdsong
and flying kites
We thank you

For high mountains
good food
and city parks
We thank you

For sea monsters
clean water
and swimming pools
We thank you

For each other's company
For this time together
For your walking with us
We thank you

Ps 104

Praise God, O my soul.
O God, my God, how great you are.
God, you have made so many things,
how wisely you have made them all.
I will sing to God all my life.
As long as I live I will sing God's praises.
May God be pleased with my song,
for my gladness comes from God.

A song ('You shall go out with joy', 'The peace of the earth' or 'May the God of peace go with us')

A closing blessing

God of the elements, bless us:
breathe on us,
wash us clean,
warm us,
root us in your good ground,
and nourish our living with holy joy. **Amen**

Ruth Burgess

Ascension

Goodbye

(Acts 1:1–11)

A monologue from a disciple, following Jesus' Ascension.

Goodbye.
He didn't actually say 'goodbye'.
He didn't say, 'I'm going now. I'm leaving you.'
He didn't ask if we were ready.
He didn't tell us, 'This is it. You won't see me again.'
He didn't even try to reassure us with,
'Everything's going to be all right.'
For once, he didn't tell us not to worry, not to be afraid;
he didn't pull us up for having such little faith.

'Stay in the city. Wait for the Spirit.'
That was it. Stay and wait.
Did he know how hard it would be to do that?
How hard it is to trust we're in the right place,
we need to stick together,
and what we've been promised will come.

There we were, full of our own agendas as usual,
thinking this was his time to overthrow the Romans.
And he shot right back at us –
no, you don't get to know the times!
How can he trust us to stay, to wait,
when we still have such half-baked ideas
about what he's all about and what he wants from us?

'You will receive power. You will be my witnesses.'
His final words.
What kind of power will it be? Will it be obvious? Will it change us?
Something will have to change
before any of us go witnessing in Samaria,
that's for sure!
But so much has already changed.

Goodbye, Lord …

goodbye to the sound of your laughter
and the look of mischief in your eyes.
Goodbye to being able to prod you
and nudge you
and just sit with you,
by the boats and under the stars and round the table.
Goodbye to watching how you do things.
Goodbye to all our clumsiness being covered by your charisma.
We can't hide behind you any more.
It's over to us now, isn't it?

And the only way you could stay, is by leaving.
And the only way you could always be here, is by going away.
It's not really goodbye, Lord, is it?
Can we trust you on that?

Jo Love, Spill the Beans

Gone

(Acts 1:1–11)

This script is best done in the style of Monty Python, and with lots of expression and pauses so that it takes some time. There should be lots of exasperation from Voice A and irritation from Voice B.

Voice A:	Gone.
Voice B:	Gone?
Voice A:	Gone!
Voice B:	Gone?!
Voice A:	Gone.
Voice B:	Where?
Voice A:	Where??

Voice B:	Where?
Voice A:	Up.
Voice B:	Up?
Voice A:	Up!
Voice B:	Up, up?
Voice A:	Up, up!
Voice B:	How?
Voice A:	How?!
Voice B:	How?
Voice A:	Just like that! *(lift hands)*
Voice B:	Just like that! *(imitating)*
Voice A:	Just like that *(repeat action)*
Voice B:	Not like that? *(arms flapping)*
Voice A:	No, not like that. Like that! *(lift arms)*
Voice B:	Like that.
Voice A:	When?
Voice B:	When??
Voice A:	Just now!
Voice B:	Now?
Voice A:	Now!!
Voice B:	Really?
Voice A:	Really!

Voice B: No, really??

Voice A: Yes, really!

Voice B: Oh!

Voice A: Oh?!

Voice B: Oh!

Voice off: People of Galilee, why do you stand looking up to heaven? This Jesus, who has been taken up from you into heaven, will come in the same way as you saw him go into heaven.

john Murning, Spill the Beans

Ascension questions

On that life-changing day
the disciples stood gazing up
waiting for something else.
Anything to show the Master hadn't
finally disappeared into a cloud
and left them.
Angels had to persuade them
he would come again.

Really?

Here we are.
Disciples in this dispensation.
Still waiting.

When will he come again?
How long, O Lord?
How long the Kingdom?

Pam Hathorn

Ascension song

(Tune: 'Aurelia')

We come to you, Lord Jesus,
with much we need to say.
In hope and love and longing,
we seek a way to pray.
We yearn for understanding,
for peace in place of fear;
assure of your presence,
show us that you are near.

The first disciples knew you;
though they had locked the door,
in Easter love you entered,
spoke words to reassure.
The hands you held out to them
disfigured by the cross,
made real the peace you offered,
born out of pain and loss.

Ascended Lord, no boundaries
of time exist for you.
Your words of peace once spoken
are for our hearing too.
A gift to heal our heartache,
a prayer phrase to recite;
your deepening peace within us
turns darkness into light.

Christ, lover of all people,
your peace we're called to share.
However life is threatened,
your peace demands we care.
Empower our search for justice,
inspire us in the quest,
till reconciled, the whole world
with Love's shalom is blest.

Avis Palmer

Ascension prayer

Jesus
risen to be with us always,
you are alive
in our hearts,
awakening hope,
inspiring faith,
empowering us
with your Spirit.

Give us the courage
to live for you.

Transform us
with your words and your ways,
that the world
might glimpse your glory
and know the wholeness of your love. Amen

Louise Gough

We see him

(A disciple reflects)

I don't really remember our journey.
It didn't seem to take very long,
yet in a way, it went on forever.
We climbed higher and higher in a mist,
then suddenly we reached the summit,
the sun broke through the clouds
and Jesus was there with us again –
our world was aglow with glory.

We wanted to ask him all sorts of questions
and get some answers to help us make sense of it all.
All he said – as he had before – was

'I'm sending you out to spread the good news
of God's love, to everyone, everywhere.'
It didn't seem strange at the time;
and it was only afterwards that we began to ask ourselves,
'How can a few ordinary people change the world?'

Earlier he had talked of loving us,
of going back to his Father – who was our Father too.
I ask you, can we call the Holy Lord of all the universe,
whose name was too sacred even to speak, 'Abba' – Dad?
But because he said it, we knew it was all right.

On that mountain we were bathed in the beauty of God,
the beauty that radiated from Jesus himself.
He was so aglow with God's love he almost shimmered.
'Don't forget,' he said, 'I am always with you,
to the end of time'; we could barely take it in.
Then the cloud came down on the mountaintop
and when it lifted, he was gone;
though something of his presence remained.

We see him all the time – in our mind's eye,
in our hearts, in the depths of our being,
and, best of all, when we talk about him;
we see Jesus in others too:
in each one of us,
in you.

Carol Dixon

Ascension of the Cosmic Christ

In the beginning was the Word,
and the Word was with God.

The eternal Cosmic Christ.
The Word.
The wisdom of God.

Matter was made first as the Word was spoken,
as the stars and planets were given birth.
The Word was with God,
and through the Word all things came into being.

In every star, every leaf, every cloud, every molecule,
is the Word, the Christ, Holy wisdom from the very beginning.
In all time, in all places, in all life was the Word,
and in one time, in one place, in one life,
a carpenter named Jesus.
In feet that felt the dust of our earth between his toes,
in a voice that could silence storms,
in hands that touched the diseased.
Word, wisdom, light.

But powers not from Word, wisdom and light,
but from coercion, force and greed,
could not stand to see the Word of God
shown in the self-giving but powerful love of a human life,
and they killed him.

But love is greater than hate,
and death could not silence the Word.

He ascends beyond the one form of matter,
into all matter.
Do not try to look beyond the clouds to see where he has gone,
because, look, he returns to you,
the Cosmic Christ,
in clouds, stars, planets, trees, gamma rays and oxygen molecules,

beyond the body of a man,
into the body of all who make their being with God.

And he is with us always,
in the expanding, evolving wonder of our cosmos.
His breath is in the air that surrounds us,
his sweat and tears in every river, every sea and every raindrop.
His voice in all who cry out in need,
his body in every piece of bread shared with the hungry.

Once again,
powers not from Word, wisdom and light,
but from coercion, force and greed,
set out to destroy the Word.
In a quest for wealth,
polluting the air and the seas,
silencing the voice of the needy,
refusing to share bread.

The eternal Cosmic Christ,
the Word, the wisdom of God
cries out again for new life,
for resurrection.
The Word refuses to be silenced,
rising to new life,
wherever flowers bloom through cracks in a wasteland,
wherever hope can be found in despair.
Once again love is greater than hate.
Where his disciples cry out for justice –
and if his disciples keep silent,
the stones of the earth will shout aloud.
Death cannot silence the Word.

Look around, and listen.
Don't look for him beyond the clouds.
He will return.

Liz Delafield

Summer in June

Thirteen orchids

It was just a few weeks ago that these familiar slopes were covered in blue
shimmering with the old bells – not those armada invaders.
Now there are odd reminders of what was there,
azure dots in a rising tide of bracken.
It always surprises me that when the bracken is on the move, it climbs so fast.
Soon it will be head-high and tracks that I know well
will become difficult as I struggle to keep my head above the green.

This morning the tide was still coming in.
I know it will get higher but bracken like the sea
has its own rhythm – it will not be high tide forever.
I counted thirteen orchids amid the green,
like cowries hiding among the pebbles.
Orchids have their season too – they come and go.
But they reminded me today that when bracken threatens to overwhelm,
there are surprises waiting to be glimpsed beneath our feet.
I must keep my eye out for orchids, treasure easy to miss.

John Randall

Ever at play in God's presence
(Proverbs 8:30–31)

God jumps in puddles with me,
laughing and splashing rainbows on the road.
God pushes me on a swing, steps back and shouts,
'Higher! Higher!'
Her giggles are infectious
and the wind blowing in our hair exhilarates.

We link arms and enter the woods,
our eyes taking it all in, the high trees, the dappled green leaves,
our beings absorb the deep silence,
occasionally punctuated by birdsong and the thrum of bees.

We come across a little pool and stop to skim stones.
God is really good. Her stones nearly reach the other bank,
while mine *shk, shk,* plop into the water.
I don't mind much. She is God.

Reaching a clearing, where the sun flits lazily,
we sit on a fallen log, making daisy chains.
It is a perfect day.
God rests her head on my shoulder and says,
'I've had fun today. Thanks.'

My heart cracks with joy.

Mary Hanrahan

Words like birds

Like ordinary garden-variety
birds around the house,
and, like them, often
in the early morning,
words sometimes sing to me.
Not obscure, Latinate ones,
but plainer ones, the robins
and sparrows of language,
words about the senses,
and what they teach,
words about the importance
of daily, domestic life:
the well-made nest,
the luscious worm,
gratuitous crumbs,
the launching of fledglings
from the nest's safety
into a dangerous world.
Like the warbling wren

who lives in the eaves,
who, as I do, rises early,
some simple words carry
a symphony of meaning
in a tiny puff of sound.

Bonnie Thurston

Why this discontent?

Of late, I gasped at beauty.
Each day small happenings,
a walk, a swim, a cycle ride,
link the past I knew
with the seeming unformed present
that is now.

May and broom,
fire and wind,
manna, holy bread.

Tendrils, sprays, royal array,
thicker, brighter for delay,
richer in our sight
against surprise of summer sky.

I touch the floating fronds
of giant cow parsley heads,
spy peeping pink campions,
white stitchwort
and the last bluebells.

Sunshine warming my shoulders,
slowing my breathing
until my whirring thoughts
tune with the whirring grasshoppers
and memories float of childhood,
of swimming in the River Avon
at Freshford and Farley Hungerford.

Summer opens the treasure store
that tells that God is good.

*'Let all things their creature bless.
And worship Him in humbleness,
Alleluia.'*

Liz Gregory-Smith

Thank you

Thank you, Creator God, for summer's warmth
and light, your gift.
Help us to joy in the promise of each day.

Thank you, Jesus, for summer's peace
and stillness, your gift.
Help us to rest in the beauty of each day.

Thank you, gentle Spirit, for summer's colour
and life, your gift.
Help us to thrive in the hope of each day.

Holy Trinity, dynamic and loving, we thank you for
seasons and cycles.
But especially for today in this season of summer.

Jean Hudson

A summer lament

'One swallow does not a summer make'*
but sometimes now
I yearn to see just one
as the summer months unfold.
I long to see the fast flight
of swallows up above –
diving, climbing, turning,
the true acrobats of the sky.

In summers past the skies were filled
with whirling, wheeling summer birds,
migrants from distant lands,
an easy tick for June birders.
The evening sky echoed
with the scream of swifts
as they turned and twisted,
feasted and fed on flies caught on the wing.

Now I sorrow at summer's empty skies,
no swallow whirling or wheeling,
no scream of swift to pierce the twilight,
just empty blue and silent sky.

God forgive me for not noticing what was going on.
God forgive me for what I've done, or not done
to protect those summer friends.
Lord, guide our caring and our living
that summer skies might be renewed.

Simon Taylor

A phrase that was apparently penned not in the British Isles, where we are always complaining about the uncertainties of our summer weather, but in Greece by Aristotle in the fourth century BC.

Feathered friends

In spite of the heat
it has been a summer
of ten species before breakfast,
increasing avian activity,
especially the week after
the banks were mowed.

Birdsong is vesper hymn,
for a solitude so fulsome
is not harmed but enhanced
by the whisper of wings,
by the broken blue egg
beneath the lilac.

Bonnie Thurston

In celebration of your creation

God of power, as the countryside reveals
opening buds and ripening grain:
We celebrate your purpose in creation.

God of salvation, as the countryside provides
tranquility and timelessness:
We celebrate your grace in creation.

God of wholeness, as the countryside sparkles
with running, living water:
We celebrate your healing in creation.

Father, Son and Holy Spirit, help us to preserve
all that gives and enhances life:
In celebration of your creation.

Jean Hudson

Appreciating the light

Gracious and merciful God,
you have given us so many
precious gifts. The clarity of day
gladdens us from dawn until dusk.
The lights of the night enable us
to see our world differently,
set as it is among the stars
and the planets of space.

Holy and life-giving Creator
of so much variety and so many dimensions,
continue to guide us towards
that enlightenment which only you
can give us to value the great and the small,
the immensity of your vision for us,
the limitations of our human views
and the ability to appreciate difference.

God of light, foresight and insight,
you have revealed to us your gift
of a perfect humanity in Christ
and invite us by your grace
to be completed by him,
the light of your Word given to us
to be reflected in us.

Terry Garley

At Alresford Creek

There are literally millions more impressive places in the world.
It's just a footpath through a copse of trees
leading down to the creek.
On either side brambles, reeds and mosses grow
in brackish,
and it must be admitted,
very smelly
mud.
You could walk straight through
without noticing anything.

But stop.
Stand still.
Wait.
Listen to barely audible rustlings and whisperings.

Do more than listen.
Feel.
Know.

Some other is here,
a more-than-self.
Beyond words,
beyond description.
Inviting worship.

This is a sacred place.
Chainsaws and bulldozers could wreck it in seconds
and another temple would be destroyed.

Brian Ford

Highland morning

On this quiet track
in early summer
amid birch and larch and pine
who could not sense the sacred
and feel creation's heart of love?

Fourteen centuries have passed
since Iona's monks –
at one with nature's pulse,
alive to crag and stream –
trod these Highland hills,
carrying the Good News about the One
whose energies of light
pulsate through strath and glen.

This track is holy ground,
a sacred space,
where, walking lightly,
wonder becomes my companion.

I look through the trees
aware of the shy deer
who has grazed here longer than centuries,
certain heir of mountain and forest.

As I meet her gaze,
something in my spirit
leaps with joy,
for I feel at one with all that lives
on this glorious Highland day.

Peter Millar

Midsummer

Twinkling stars slowly fade,
sky lights.
An early bird rises, spreads its wings
and flies off into the endless horizon.
A chorus of birdsongs fills the air.
The gathered people connect hands and form a circle,
voices join in a soft humming.
Lighter and brighter, the rising of the sun.
Rays touch the sacred space
through the standing stones left by the Ancient Ones,
our elders in time past.
The circle rejoices as we are touched by light,
the warmth of the sun awakening the love in our hearts.
In gratitude for the old way,
we spread our own wings as we enter the dawn of a new day.

Roberta van Biezen

Summer solstice

This is a sequence we use as a family to celebrate the summer solstice, with each willing member taking a verse.

The fire is lit.

The longest day is here once more
and we are here again
to celebrate with all our kin
in fire and food and wine.

The longest day is here once more.
The fire once more alight.
Six months since the shortest day
inched slowly from our sight.

January brought the cold,
our gardens were asleep.
The downs sat sullen in the snow
with huddled chills of sheep.

February's flood and wind
tore across the land.
The sea roared in and flung its waves
up on the battered strand.

March saw shoots begin to thrive,
leaves and buds were rife
and in the woods the birds' new song
heralded new life.

April's sun warmed up the earth,
springing now with flowers,
squirrels danced along the hedge
oblivious to the showers.

Jack has danced, and Jack is dead
and yet he lives once more:
his seed is sown, his crops will grow
to fill our summer store.

Midsummer comes, the sun is high,
its warmth and light abound.
It fills the earth with promise
as it penetrates the ground.

Midsummer comes, the air is clear,
the roses are in bloom,
the earth shows off its riches
though they are gone too soon.

Another year, another fire,
no reason to be glum,
as we give thanks for what has been
and what is yet to come.

Another fire, another year,
another glass to raise
in thanks that we are who we are
as we turn another page.

The longest day is here again,
the solstice fire burns bright.
We revel in the warmth it brings
as we share love and light.

Brian Hick

Pentecost

Welcome, Holy Spirit

Welcome, Holy Spirit,
we celebrate your presence.

Welcome, Comforter,
touch our souls with your peace.

Welcome, Awakener,
touch our souls with your life.

Welcome, Disturber,
touch our souls with your truth.

Lady Wisdom,
you waken us to the truth of God;
fan the fire of holy love,
teach us the best way,
and comfort us –
in distress or failure.
May our worship
honour your presence
among us.
Amen

Chris Polhill

When the day of Pentecost had come

'When the day of Pentecost had come, they were all together in one place.' (Acts 2:1, NIV)

It had been a strange few weeks.
Jesus had told us to stay in Jerusalem
and to wait for the power that the Holy Spirit would give us.
All the disciples were here
(except for Judas, who had killed himself),
and over a hundred followers of Jesus,
and we had all gathered together

on the morning of the Feast of Pentecost.
As well as all the people living in Jerusalem,
there were thousands of visitors
as this was a pilgrimage holiday
to celebrate the giving of the Torah,
and to thank God for the harvest.

It's difficult to describe to you what happened.
All of sudden there was a loud noise –
it sounded like a wind had come right inside the house –
a strong wind, the sort that can cause real damage,
and when we looked at each other
we could see flames, real flames, hovering over each other's heads,
and it felt like something was filling us up,
filling us up with wonder and love and joy.

We came out of the house into the crowded street.
We were praising God –
we were talking and laughing and crying.
Whatever it was that had happened to us
it was amazing.
It felt really good.

We must have been making quite a noise,
as people stopped and listened to us,
people from all over
from Mesopotamia and Egypt,
from Cappadocia and Libya and Crete.
And somehow they could all understand
what we were saying,
even though they all spoke different languages;
it was really odd.

People began asking questions,
some people thought we were drunk,
and Peter knew that he had to say something,
and he got up
and began to preach.

John Murning, Spill the Beans

Finding the right words

Have you ever met a person who speaks a different language to you?

Have you ever travelled in a country where people speak a different language to you?

Are you learning to speak another language at school?

Have you ever watched a film with subtitles in another language?

Some languages have a different alphabet to ours.

Do you know any?

Look at examples.

Some languages are read in different ways: across, or up and down a page.

Do you know any?

Look at examples.

Some places have different languages.

Can you think of words we use in church that we don't use in the shops or in school?

Books are written in many languages. The books in the Old Testament, or First Testament part of the Bible, are written in Hebrew. The books in the New Testament are written in Greek. For us to be able to understand them someone has translated them into the language we speak.

Today is a day that the church calls Pentecost. The story of what happened to the followers of Jesus on the day of Pentecost is in a book called the Acts of the Apostles in the New Testament. It's a strange story. You might like to listen to it and see what you make of it.

The writer was trying to describe something unusual that had happened and it was hard for him to find the right words.

Sometimes, if people can't find the right words, they use pictures or music instead. Lots of painters have tried to paint a picture of the day of Pentecost.

Have a look on Google Images and see what you can find.

Note: Have examples of different languages and alphabets available. If you don't have Internet access where you meet, print out some pictures of the Feast of Pentecost beforehand. You might also want to explore some songs and music for Pentecost.

Ruth Burgess, Spill the Beans

The beautiful noise of God

Suddenly
the shocked silence
of crucifixion,
resurrection,
shattered.

Into that
waiting
prayerful
hopeful space
the symphony
of the Spirit
boomed.

Formerly fearful disciples
gifted with the power of speech
transcending the boundaries of language:
God is for all!

Those drawn
by the sounds
of the Spirit
heard
and understood.

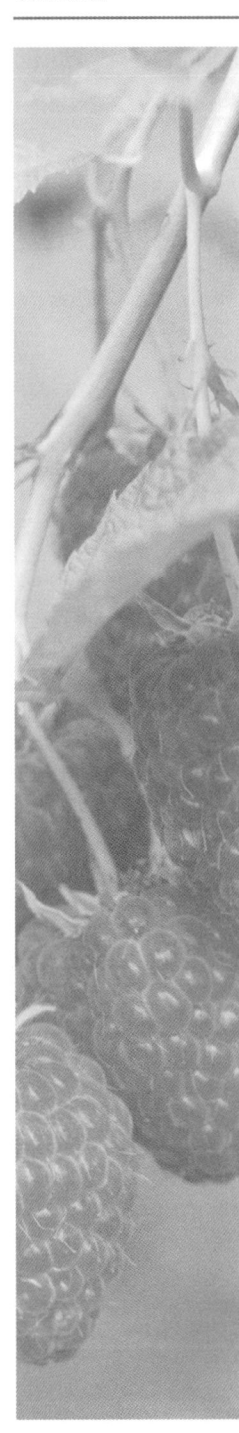

Raised voices
reverberating hearts
lives transformed …

The beautiful noise
of God.

Louise Gough

A brand-new day

Let us give thanks
for a brand-new day,
a festival day,
a holy day,
a restful day,
a Pentecost day.

Let us give thanks
for renewal,
regeneration,
revival.

Let us give thanks
for inspiration,
hope,
love
and praise.

Let us give thanks
for babies and toddlers,
children and young adults,
middle-aged and old folk –
all the people of God.

Let us give thanks
for the church,
its buildings,

its history,
its sense of community.
Let us give thanks
for ministers and missionaries,
craftsmen and artists,
engineers and chemists
who have made a difference to our world.

Let us give thanks
for the Holy Spirit,
God's gift to us
on this special day.
Amen

John Murning, Spill the Beans

Come, Holy Spirit

Come, Holy Spirit,
into the areas of our lives
where there is darkness
when there should be light;
where there is anger
and we find it difficult
to forgive those who,
maybe unintentionally,
have hurt us.

Come, Holy Spirit,
into the areas of our lives
where there are problems
and we need your wisdom
about how to solve them;
where we are uncertain
and we need your guidance
about the way we
should proceed.

Come, Holy Spirit,
into the areas of our lives
where there is sadness
and we need your comfort;
where there is pain and hurt
and we need your healing;
where we are afraid
and we need your courage
to empower us.

Come, Holy Spirit,
into the areas of our lives
where we are reluctant
to grant you entry
in case you want to make
too many changes;
where we know we are weak
and we need your power
to make us strong.

Come, Holy Spirit …

Kathy Crawford

Big Spirit

Big Spirit,
colourful Spirit,
noisy Spirit,
energy of God.
Hear us as we pray.

You dreamt up the shapes of creation,
making a world of blue and green,
and we thank you.

You chose the colours for the rainbow;
you paint it across the sky,
and we thank you.

You make us restless for a new world,
willing us to work for peace,
and we thank you.

You challenge us to break down barriers,
to form friendships
with those others ignore,
and we thank you.

You get angry when
people are treated unfairly,
calling us to love everyone,
and we thank you.

You give us words to communicate
and music with which to sing them,
and we thank you.

Big Spirit,
colourful Spirit,
noisy Spirit,
energy of God.
Hear us as we pray.
So be it. Amen

Roddy Hamilton, Spill the Beans

Mystery gift

In the centre of worship, place a large taped-up cardboard box with posting labels stuck on its sides, the address label bearing the name of your congregation, church and the street address.

You could follow this piece up with a short discussion time, asking people what excites them, and what scares or puzzles them, about the gift of the Spirit.

A gift … with our name on it.
Hmm … who's it from? …
Sender: God.
Oh! And what's this? …

Contents:
Undiluted Holy Spirit.
Additives and preservatives:
Divine adoption,
inheritance of eternal joy.
Expiry date:
Never.

Danger:
Hazardous material.
Highly flammable.
Do not handle with care or caution.
No licence required.
Do use if the seal is broken and contents have leaked.
Do use without supervision.
Do eat, drive,
operate machinery,
use your mobile phone,
while using this product.

Recommended daily dose:
As much as you can take.
May vary.
Suitable for children under 3 years,
wheelchair users,

vegetarians,
allergy sufferers,
elderly people,
pregnant women.

Possible side effects:
May cause alertness,
empowerment,
loss of control,
compulsion to step outside of comfort zones,
enhanced empathy,
substantial hearing gain,
prophetic wisdom.

Use liberally in affected areas
to alleviate symptoms of injustice, exploitation and greed.
Directions:
After absorbing healthy dose,
sprinkle or pour externally.
Increased effectiveness with increased use.

If undelivered:
Keep knocking gently until intended recipient opens up.

Jo Love, Spill the Beans

Wild Spirit of God

Wild Spirit of God,
come refresh and restore us!
Blow through our tiredness,
disturb our dull routines,
awaken our expectations,
alert us to your presence,
excite our faith,
until the fire of your love
takes hold in us again
and your Pentecost light
warms every heart
and draws others to you,
the source of all life and joy.
Amen

Louise Gough

Dependency

A prayer written before my ordination as a deacon.

Lord, you have called me
to be the one who others will depend upon.
May I prove dependable,
not in my own strength,
but because you work through me.
Give me courage to hold the hands
that reach out and grasp for another to hold.
And as I reach for those hands,
may I hold out your nail-pierced hands.

Lord, many followed you
because they saw you as one
who would release them from the tyranny
of political oppression.

Lord, many will try to depend upon me
as one who can bear the pain of their living.
Give me the perception and strength not to reject
but to offer instead your nail-pierced hands.

Lord, you know my frailty,
weakness and brokenness.
May I serve you in you
and draw my strength from your broken body.
May my still-point be found in you,
your being be the ground of my being.
But let me never forget
that the gentle Holy Spirit comes
in wind and tongues of fire.

S Anne Lawson

Without a word

The wind has many voices:
she can howl;
she can whisper;
she can shriek;
she can sigh;
she can whistle.
Without a word,
the wind has many voices.

And she goes where she pleases:
blowing away cobwebs;
bringing down trees;
picking up sand grains;
rustling leaves;
cooling a hot day;
biting through layers of winter warmth;
shifting clouds;
pushing at our backs;

throwing rain at our faces;
stirring up waves;
stretching out sails;
bending grass;
tugging at flags;
dislodging roof tiles;
rattling windows;
turning turbines.
Fierce.
Exciting.
Refreshing.
Caressing.
Breath of creation.
Uncontrollable.

The breath in our bodies has many voices:
gasps of relief;
groans of despair;
whoops of excitement;
gulps of shock;
grunts of displeasure;
moans of grief;
guffaws of laughter;
wails of pain;
gasps of delight.
Without a word,
our breath has many voices.

Prayer has many voices.
The Spirit without meets the spirit within.
Wind and breath in sighs and squalls,
Spirit blowing where she will.

No words needed.

Jo Love, Spill the Beans

Spirit of Life

Spirit of Life,
you hovered over the waters at the world's beginning,
and hover over us still.
As creation continues with this brand-new day,
all creatures join our hymn of praise.

Spirit of God, present with us now.
Alleluia, alleluia.

Divine Advocate,
you stand alongside us,
you defend and council us in times of trouble,
you enable and empower us to stand firm against injustice.

Spirit of God, present with us now.
Alleluia, alleluia.

Holy Fire,
burning within our hearts,
the gentle embers of a soft and comforting warmth,
a tiny flame seeming precarious amid the darkness,
or a raging inferno that challenges and changes.
The same fire, burning within each one.

Spirit of God, present with us now.
Alleluia, alleluia.

Breath of God,
your soft kiss touches us gently as we sleep,
your howling gale rattles at our windows.
You blow where you will, often in unexpected places.
You encircle us with the whirlwind of your love.

Spirit of God, present with us now.
Alleluia, alleluia.

Liz Delafield

Light me, Lord

Light me, Lord:
Let me sense the wings
stretched over everything;
let me glimpse the face
behind the galaxies;
let my mind
find itself aligned
with the unending thought
that moved, and taught
emptiness to form a word;
let the desires
that hold me
night-bound here
blaze in your fire:
because my darkness
needs a presence.
Light me, Lord.

Roddy Cowie

A Eucharistic prayer for Pentecost

Before life stirred
your Spirit brooded over darkness
exploding light in all directions.

**Rainbow promise
celebrated your creation.**

Your Spirit led a people
to long for you;

**guiding them gently:
a pillar of cloud by day;
fire by night.**

Prophets spoke of your justice
dancing Spirit songs of liberation;

with tambourine and whispered hope.

Your still small voice
in lonely places;

**as dry bones lived
and friendships blossomed.**

With tender Spirit passion
you embodied Love
nestling in the womb of Mary;

**calling fishermen,
accompanying women,
blessing children.**

They found themselves on Calvary's road
accompanying Love
to the cross
and the tomb;
meeting Love in the garden
and on the shore;

**taking the risk of letting go
so the Spirit of comfort might
come to them.**

Accompanying Christ today in one another
with life-giving encounters of grace,
we flesh out the Spirit's fruit
through Spirit gifts
in communities of hope;

**celebrating the gifts of others
sustaining us on our journeys;
our hearts burn within us
as we feel the stirrings of your presence.**

Touch us by your Spirit
as we touch this bread and wine,
fruits of the earth to nourish us with
the very presence of Christ;
as we recall the night of betrayal
after he had washed the feet of his companions,
when Jesus blessed bread,
breaking it and
sharing it, saying,
'This is my body which is given for you;
do this to re-member me.'

We recall the moment
after supper
when Jesus blessed the cup
he gave to them, saying,
'Drink this
all of you;
this is my blood
of the new promise
shed for you
and for many
for the forgiveness of sin;
do this as often

as you drink it
to re-member me.'

Blazing Spirit,
light these gifts
with holy fire,
so we who receive them
may be ablaze with your love.
As we re-member
fractured stories
of your marred image,
broken bodies of inhospitality
and blood spilt in war and waste,
do not leave us in a place
of loneliness;

do not abandon us.

Come as comforter and counsellor;
come as fiery dragon's breath;
come lightly as dove's wings;

come make your home in us.

In this humble meal
we receive you;
in our embodied hospitality
you take your refuge;
when your wings are broken
and your fire quenched.

Come Spirit,
yearn for us
as we yearn for you.
Together we shall burst
the bars of fear,
flying freely,
bringing warmth to the earth
and winds of justice
to those who cry 'Peace'.

The breaking and sharing of the Bread

The Spirit calls us to break down the walls of division;
to break through the barriers of fear;
to break out of our tombs of apathy.
So we break this bread as a symbol of solidarity
with all communities who work and pray to this end.
This is our unity with all that breathes the Spirit of God,
and our commitment to embody
the fruit and gifts of Pentecost.

Post-Communion prayer

Spiralling Spirit,
through this meal
ground us in community
with compassionate welcome
to all who touch the threshold of this place.

Dare us to proclaim
your disturbing power
and summer glory
in the harshness
of the world's winter.

Blessing

Come, revealing Spirit,
bless our unfurling
within your presence,
gathering us closely
into your soft down of peace
with blessings of love
and joyfulness of hope
as we continue our pilgrimage
of becoming Spirit-filled.
Alleluia.

Alleluia, Alleluia,
thanks be to God.

Elizabeth Baxter

Holy Spirit – the comforter

When you are there,
when I notice,
there is a smile in my soul,
of recognition,
of welcome,
of love.

My heart dances
and I move
with the wind of your sending,
feet light as air,
free to feel
your joy.

In your presence
is deep comfort
and everything pauses.
I am absorbed,
I am held,
in peace.

Chris Polhill

Holy Spirit – the disturber

Lady Wisdom,
I wish I had listened to you,
followed the nudge,
found the courage
to take
a different direction.

I said I would follow you,
running a risk,
ready to roll
with the
free-flowing currents
of air and opinion.

Instead I played safe,
went to the known,
stayed with security,
losing opportunity
and the path
promised.

Chris Polhill

Whitsunday service

Look at the pews on Pentecost, and see,
under the beams from the high window-panes,
flame upon flame shining out brilliantly,
dancing to greet its fellow-flames again.
As the tired mouths repeat words often said,
and ageing hands struggle to find the place,
fire rises round their shoulders and their heads,
lit, and sustained, by God's unwavering grace.

Whether their eyes look up, or stay cast down;
whether they battle the fierce doubts of youth,
or drift towards the comfort of dark ground;

whether they know or not, this is the truth:
to those on whom God's living flame once falls,
blessing is given: and it is not recalled.

Roddy Cowie

For your Spirit

For your Spirit at work in creation,
in the growing, breathing and moving of life
on our beautiful planet Earth.
Thanks be to God.

For your Spirit working through history,
in the poor hearing good news, in captives seeking liberty
and in eyes opened to new ways of seeing.
Thanks be to God.

For your Spirit at work in your church,
in traditions that root us
and in challenges that move us.
Thanks be to God.

For the unexpected people and places through which your Spirit is moving,
in all those moved by compassion,
strengthened with courage and comforted with hope.
Thanks be to God.

For the gifts of the Spirit evident here today –
for music, art, hospitality, preaching, flower arranging,
serving tea and nurturing children.*
Thanks be to God.

For the future to which you are calling us,
for the challenges and joys for which you have chosen us.
Thanks be to God.

Liz Delafield

*Adapt to include particular gifts in your community

Transformative Spirit

I don't think I like what is happening.
It's something new, and strange,
and I don't like change!

Now, I was there.
I witnessed the tongues of fire touching people –
and I had to duck a few times to avoid bursting into flames!

Well, at least that's what I thought would happen!
Yet nobody set themselves on fire that day;
they did not combust,
as you would have expected,
but it seemed that something inside them changed.

Take John as an example.
He was always so cautious,
so wanting to do the right thing,
that it almost paralysed him.

Bartholomew always seemed to be hiding,
the kind of man who could disappear into the background
whenever Jesus was looking for volunteers in the mission field.

Thomas questioned everything,
and would not believe until he saw proof
that something actually worked.

And now they have all changed.
It is as if the fear inside of them disappeared.
They stopped talking about what they should do next
and went out and just started telling people about Jesus!
They spoke clearly and with conviction,
they did everything Jesus told them to do,
like healing the sick,
feeding the hungry,
caring for the needy,
welcoming children and women into the movement,
and forgiving people for their wrongs

so that they could have a fresh start.
And it seemed to work.

I know it's difficult to understand,
but they were energised,
free and open,
loving and honest,
focused on the Kingdom that Jesus had spoken about.
It was like they were actually building the Kingdom,
person by person,
act by act,
word by word.
They showed no fear of the religious authorities,
refused to hide any longer from the Roman soldiers
and they made themselves available to everyone.

And now I feel like I have missed out on something special.
Why did I duck and dive and avoid the Spirit of God?
What was I so afraid of that I hid away?

Change, I was afraid of change.
I like things as they are.
I like to play life safe, and by the rules,
but the Spirit of God is no respecter of the rules.
She seems to care not a hoot for good order and planning;
she just seems to work where she's needed:
liberates people from the life they had
into this new and lively and vibrant
way of doing the things of God.
And it is undoubtedly the power of God at work
in ordinary men and women,
just like Jesus had promised to us.
The Holy Spirit would be his parting gift to us he said –
and I missed her!

Yet … I guess it's never too late to change,
even an old stick in the mud like me.

O Lord, pour out your Spirit upon me.

John Murning, Spill the Beans

It's not how I would have done it

It's not how I would have done it,
the most important event in world history:
the God/man returning to life.
And nobody saw it happen.
It took place inside a sealed tomb.
When the stone was moved aside
the only witnesses were a few terrified guards,
later bribed to lie about it.
The first person to see the risen Christ
was a woman.
In a patriarchal, misogynistic society
how much weight does her testimony have?
And it was a strange way to say goodbye.
He just blessed us
and then disappeared.
No bands of angels to welcome him home.
No voice from heaven congratulating him
on a job perfectly done.
Just two blokes telling us that he's going to return
someday.
And do you know what he told us to do?
Wait,
just wait.
Some of the lads were pretty disappointed,
doubtful.
What a downbeat ending.

It was so weird that I don't understand it.
No one does.
We burst out onto the street,
working-class Galileans most of us,
gabbling nonsense.
Some said we were speaking in foreign languages.
Could be.
I didn't understand a word.

Funny way to start a new religion.
It's not how I would have done it.
But I'm not God,
luckily.

Brian Ford

Trinity

Opening responses for Trinity Sunday

Praise the God of creation:
who made us to be in relationship.

Praise the Christ of love:
who calls us friends.

Praise the Spirit of peace:
who enables us to live in unity.

Simon Taylor

Prayer of approach for Trinity Sunday

God, who has made our world with its beauty and wonder,
full of delights for us to explore,
grant us wisdom to live gently on the earth,
holding sacred the air and water, soil and sun.

God, who has called human beings your children,
made to share in the work of creation,
grant us wisdom to live in harmony with one another,
holding sacred your image in everyone.

God, whose Spirit dwells within us,
giving us power to live in your name,
grant us wisdom to discern your presence,
holding sacred the glory of love in the everyday. Amen

Jan Berry

The disciples
(Matthew 28:16–20)

Disciples,
that's what we were called:
learners, beginners, pupils, trainees.

Jesus had called twelve of us,
to travel with him, to listen to him,
to watch and learn from him.
We were an odd mixture:
different occupations, different temperaments,
different ideas about the world, about each other, about God.
But he had taught us well;
we had learnt to trust God to give us hands to heal
and words to say.
Despite a few fierce arguments,
we had mostly learnt to work together, to trust each other,
to listen and pray.

And now, at his bidding,
we were back in Galilee
at the top of a mountain.
Eleven of us now,
for Judas had gone his own way.
Mountains are special places in our history:
Noah high and dry on Ararat,
Moses on Sinai,
and Jesus had often taught us and many others
sitting down on a mountainside.

Jesus had been crucified
and buried in a tomb –
and was alive again –
people had seen him,
spoken with him
and now he was here with us
on this mountain.

We met him there as individuals,
because, although we were all his disciples,
we were still very different people.
Some of us wanted to worship him,
others of us had doubts and questions
about what had happened to him
and who he was.

And he spoke with us,
and he told us that it was time for us
to go and teach people all about him.
It was time for us to call other people
to be learners and pupils and trainees,
to call people everywhere to be disciples.
We were to baptise them
in the name of God, the Father,
and Jesus and the Holy Spirit.
We were to teach them
as we had been taught:
to love God with everything they had –
heart, mind, body, soul and spirit –
and to love their neighbours as themselves.

Those were some of the last things that Jesus said to us.
Challenging things,
words spoken with authority.
And then he said to us
that there was something else we needed to remember,
and I always have.
These were his last words;
they have always helped me and blessed me,
and I share them now with you.

Jesus said:
'Remember, I am always with you
to the end of time.'
Amen

Ruth Burgess, Spill the Beans

Saying goodbye
(Matthew 28:16–20)

Class Three were saying goodbye to their teacher. When they came back after the summer holidays she wouldn't be there. Mrs Young was moving. She was going to teach in a small school on an island in the Hebrides in Scotland.

Class Three were sad. They had enjoyed having Mrs Young as a teacher. They had done exciting projects and she told great stories. She knew that they were all different: that Jimmy had a pet rabbit and didn't like doing sums, and that Fiona loved painting and was learning to play the piano, and that Martin had a new baby sister who was called Emily Jane. She had taught them how to work in pairs and groups, to share their ideas and skills with each other. She had encouraged them to work things out for themselves and to ask for help when they needed it. And she had taught them that it wasn't the end of the world when you tried something out and it didn't work, because that was another way of learning about things.

After the holidays Class Three would be Class Four. There would be a lot of children in the school who would be younger than them. On her last afternoon with them Mrs Young had told Class Three that there was something she wanted to tell them.

Class Three listened. Mrs Young said she was going to ask each one of them to tell her and the class one thing that they had learnt this year that they could say or do to help each other and the younger children in the school.

Class Three had lots of ideas. Here are some of them:

I could sometimes play with the younger ones in the playground.

I'm good at reading. I could read stories on wet playtimes.

I can say sorry when I've hurt someone.

I can bring flowers from my garden for the classroom.

I could try not to talk so much and listen a bit more.

I could join the school choir.

Mrs Young smiled. She told Class Three that if they did all these things they would enjoy being Class Four in the school. She told them that when she had settled into her new home and school she would write to them, and perhaps they might like to write to her and her new pupils. She would not see them each day but she would still think about them.

Then it was time to say goodbye. There were smiles and tears. And then Class Three went home for their summer holidays.

Share stories of saying goodbye to teachers, class members, family members, friends.

Tell the story of Jesus saying goodbye to his disciples (Matthew 28:16–20).

Ruth Burgess, Spill the Beans

Awesome Trinity

- A: When we think of the Trinity, sometimes we concentrate on the wrong words.

- B: We think we have to try to follow the word 'Trinity' with lots of other words

- C: that will help to explain what that word means.

- D: But that never works too well because the words we use aren't big enough.

- A: So we thought it would be a better idea

B: to use words *in front* of the word 'Trinity',

C: rather than after the word 'Trinity',

D: that might help us, not so much to understand, but to bring the Trinity to life a little more.

A: So how about the words 'awesome Trinity'?

B: Or 'breathtaking Trinity'?

C: Perhaps the word 'mind-blowing' helps?

D: Or even the word 'magnificent'?

A: We thought these were pretty good words.

B: Some said we had perhaps overused our thesauruses,

C: but we needed a thesaurus to help us with words like …

D: extravagant, phenomenal and inconceivable.

A: And we also came up with other words we might use:

B: like 'intimidating',

C: or 'frightening',

D: or even 'shocking'.

A: Because the Trinity is not always cosy:

B: take Moses on the mountain,

C: or Elijah in his cave,

D: or Isaiah at his calling.

A: But we could also think of modern words like:

B: 'Unreal',

C: 'Wicked',

D: 'Ace'.

A: Because the Trinity is well up-to-date:

B: look at creation, always evolving;

C: or consider the church, always changing;

D: or wonder about community, always finding new ways to engage.

A: It seems that

B: the words we used before 'Trinity'

C: were often more important

D: than the ones we used after 'Trinity'.

A: They have more expectation,

B: more questions,

C: more colour,

D: more wonder.

A: So choose your own words:

B: be adventurous,

C: be interesting,

D: be unusual,

A: because if there is one thing we have found about the Trinity –

B: it's not always what you expect.

C: It's not all sewn up,

D: and there are dozens of words that could describe it. How would *you* describe what no one yet has been able to?

Spill the Beans

Three in One

God of the Trinity, bless us.

God of space, sea and sky,
of cloud, sun and rainbow,
of oak, leaf and acorn,
of candle, flame and wax,
of handshake, smile, embrace,
of storm, flood and rainbow,
of journey, pause and destination,
of spring, river and ocean,
of pebble, rock and cliff face,
of mirror, reflection and mystery,
of flower, petal and stamen,
of dance, song and merriment,
of country, continent and borders,
of gold, diamond and cobalt,
of industry, office and school,
of sleep, dream and rest,
of butterscotch, honey and meringue,
of word, sentence and praise,
of yarn, stitch and tapestry,
of pollen, honey and mead,
of head, arm and heart,
of computer, spreadsheet and Twitter,
of moment, days and eternity.

God of the Trinity, bless us.

Judy Dinnen

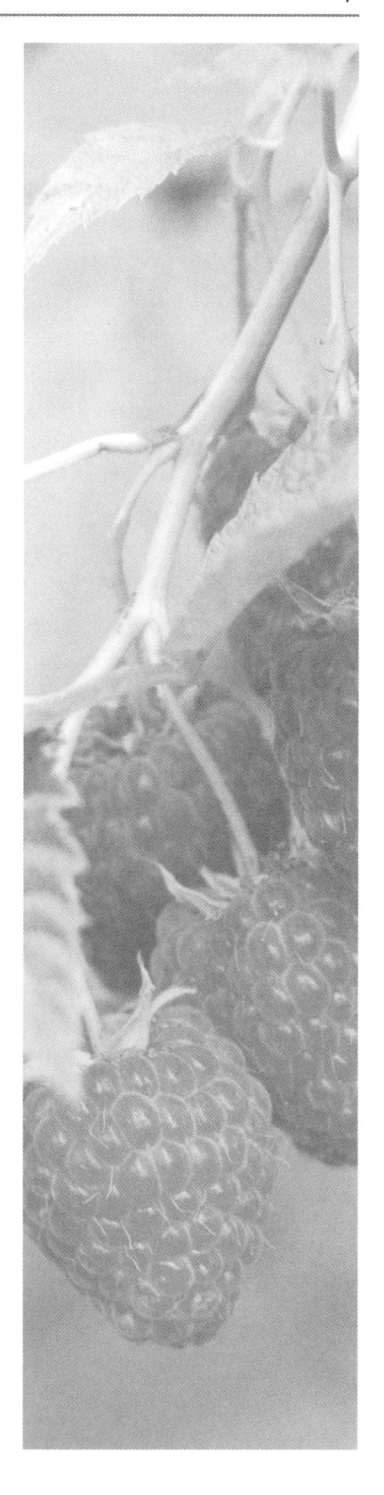

In the world, God's love declaring

(Tune: 'Blaenwern')

In the world, God's love declaring,
Wisdom dances in delight;
all earth's hope and passion sharing,
ways and truths beyond our sight.
In creation's heavenly glory
all the power of love is shown.
In the telling of earth's story,
God's redeeming grace is known.

When we reach out to the stranger,
offering welcome and embrace,
then the Christ of cross and manger
shines in every human face.
In our hands outstretched in greeting
all the strength of love is shown;
in the openness of meeting,
Christ's compassion is made known.

In our search for fairer giving
we discern the Spirit's call.
In the struggle for just living
God demands no less than all.
In our speaking, in our doing
all the hope of love is known;
in our dream of earth's renewing
Holy Wisdom shall be known.

Jan Berry

Trinity of grace

(A responsive prayer of praise)

Gracious God,
Father, Son and Holy Spirit,
you created us in love
and hold this world forever within your care.
Trinity of grace:
we put our trust in you.

Parent God,
you speak to us with words of mercy and kindness,
words that we can build our lives upon.
Your power would make us tremble
if we did not know that you are love.
Trinity of grace:
we put our trust in you.

You have drawn near to us in Jesus, Son of God;
he has come to be our light and our hope.
In Jesus, we know forgiveness of our sin
and a peace that no other can give.
Trinity of grace:
we put our trust in you.

And by the Holy Spirit you still come to us today,
giving life, inspiring justice, bringing reconciliation;
the breath of creation here with us now,
the nearness of God to give us courage and comfort.
Trinity of grace:
we put our trust in you.

Gracious God,
you promise that you will never leave us or forsake us
and that in all times and in all places we can look to you.
Nothing in life or death, on earth or in heaven
can take away the love that you have shown us in Christ Jesus.
Trinity of grace:
we put our trust in you. Amen

Simon Taylor

Trinity talk

This monologue is suitable for, but not confined to, an all-age setting.

A woman is sitting darning a hole in a jumper. She chats to a grandchild (aged about six). She sings softly, half humming:

'Holy, holy, holy, merciful and mighty,
God in three persons, blessed Trinity.'

Pass Grandma the scissors, would you, love? Handles towards me, remember. Thank you.

The song? It's one we sang in church today. Try it with me?

'Holy, holy, holy, merciful and mighty,
God in three persons, blessed Trinity.'

No, it doesn't mean 'holey' like the holes I'm darning! It's 'holy' – h-o-l-y … What does that mean? Well, it's a special word for 'good'. Like saying 'God is good'.

Miss Smith says 'good' isn't enough, does she? You have to be 'excellent'?

All right, then God is 'excellent'. But the song wouldn't work with 'excellent, excellent, excellent', would it?

Does it have to be three times? That's to fit the second line 'God in three persons, blessed Trinity'.

No, 'blessed' isn't a naughty word there. That's the right way to use it – like 'very happy'. OK, Grandma does sometimes say it when she's cross, but never mind.

What's 'Trinity'? Well, that's a bit hard to explain ... No, it's not what Granddad gets in his ears – that's tinnitus. Trinity is to do with three. It starts with T-r-i. Do you know another three word that starts like that? ... Yes, 'triangle' – well done!

Why don't we sing 'blessed Triangle'? ... You're right, it would fit the tune. But God isn't a thing, or an idea, like a triangle, He's personal. When we say our prayers we're talking to Him.

The song says 'God in three persons'. That's Father God, and Jesus, and the Holy Spirit – different, but all the one God.

Tom's got to draw three gods for homework, has he? That'll be the Greek gods – he told me about going to a museum to see statues of them. That's not the same at all. In old times in Greece people thought there were lots of gods, who had rows with each other. They weren't at all united.

'Trinity United' – a football team with just three? That's closer, but it doesn't sound quite right.

Why does the song say 'three persons'? Miss Smith would put a cross by that? It should be 'three people'? Well, yes, usually it should, but this is an exception.

What's an exception? It's when there are rules but sometimes things don't fit them. God's so special that words don't really fit Him – even with pictures and music added.

So can you tell Miss Smith that it's OK to make mistakes if you're writing about God? No – or maybe yes. There, I've finished this now – let's go and find a biscuit.

Kit Walkham

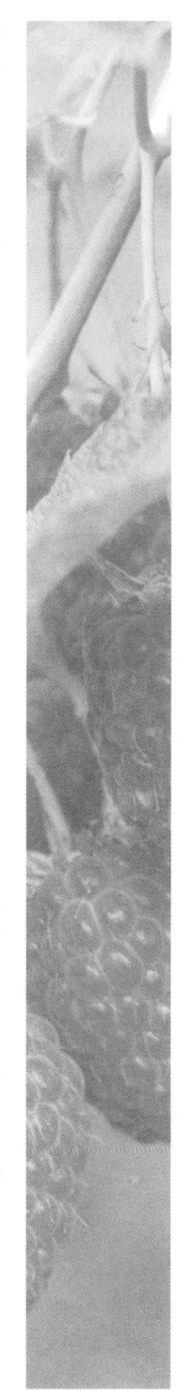

I am Alpha and Omega

I am Alpha.
I was here in the beginning; the beginning of all that is.
Before the world was, I was here, waiting, waiting for you.
Before there was sea, or crushing waves;
before there was sky, or rushing clouds;
before there was land, or snow-covered mountains,
I was here.

I was here in the beginning.
Before fish swam, or insects crawled;
before cockerels crowed, or lions roared;
before the singing of a million feathered life forms
greeted the rising sun,
I was here.

I am Alpha.
I was here before man or woman came into being.
Before you built your homes;
before you worked the fields, or subdued the land;
before you discovered technology,
or sought to control the world through science,
I was here.
I was here in the beginning,
before you lived or loved;
before you talked or toiled;
before your worried weariness made you doubt my existence,
I was here waiting, waiting for you.

I am Alpha.
There is nothing I have not seen;
there is nowhere I have not been.
There is nothing I do not know, or have not experienced.
There is no situation that I have not encountered,
there is no emotion that I do not have;
no feeling that I cannot understand.
There is no joy too great; no laughter too loud;

no amusement that I cannot enjoy;
no caring touch I cannot feel.

I was here in the beginning.
There is no sorrow I cannot share;
no tears too deep; no pain too great;
no aching loneliness that I have not known;
no hatred or betrayal that I have not suffered.
Nothing is new to me.
Before the world began, I was here waiting,
waiting for you.
I am Alpha. Before the world was, I AM.

I am Omega.
I am the end.
The end of all that was; the end of all that will be.
I am the last, the final curtain.
When the world is no more and all is still,
I'll be there waiting, waiting for you.

I am Omega,
when the sun no longer shines and the rain ceases;
when mists no longer gather, nor snowflakes fall;
when the wind stops its constant roaming
and rainbows are but a distant memory,
I'll be there.
When wheat no longer grows, nor kestrels dive;
when boats no longer sail, nor passengers arrive;
when your loud music ceases and all is hushed,
I'll be there waiting, waiting for you.

I am Omega.
When you have done your worst to destroy my world,
pulled down my trees and flattened my forests,
polluted my rivers and plundered the land,
altered the genes and confused the life cycles,
I'll be there.
When you have exploded your bombs and fought your wars,
race against race; colour against colour;

when you have abused the young and ridiculed the old;
when you have ignored the poor
and disobeyed my teaching,
I'll be there waiting, waiting for you.

I am Omega.
I am the end.
One day I will return and take you with me.
You need not fear me, for I love you.
I created you in my image,
made you to live in my world,
to know its joys and its woes.
To work; to play; to love;
to win; to lose and to start again.
To live and breathe and know that I am your God
and that you are my people.
I am the end.
When evil is banished and all creation is at peace again
as it was in the beginning,
I'll be there.

For I am Alpha and Omega.
The beginning and the end.
The first and the last.
And I am waiting, waiting for you.

Gill Bailey

Season of Trinity

Safe to worship what I do not understand,
the life of Jesus to explore slowly
through the summer months:
the one who died and rose again,
present and absent every day,
alongside amazing beauty.

Liz Gregory-Smith

God Beyond, God Within and God Between

God, for me, is the spirit dimension, inherent in everything and everyone, including me and you. It is a way of understanding which goes in the opposite direction to the 'away' God who is separate and distinct. To try to unpack this belief, I speak of 'God Beyond', 'God Within' and 'God Between'.

When I speak of God Beyond, God Within and God Between, I am not talking about the nature, the substance or the essence of a Being I might call God. God the Father, Son and Holy Spirit, I have been taught, are all persons in the orthodox Trinity, whereas for me, God Beyond, God Within and God Between are phrases by which I point to the different ways I 'experience' God. Even though God is not a person, my experience of God is still very personal.

God Beyond

I begin with God Beyond. Other people, trees, ants, rocks, moon, stars, galaxies, atoms, molecules, microbes, bacteria ... are outside, beyond me. Life is not limited to my life.

My belief is that God Beyond is the mystery in which all things hold together. I experience God Beyond as the glue which enlivens the universe.

This is my experience of the world, the universe; God Beyond. For me, God Beyond can never be thought of as a person. That is far too limiting.

God Within

I have the human experience of God Within, the experience of God within me. This is where I experience that God is love, all-encompassing and all-challenging, costly, surrounding, accepting love.

As soon as I think of God Within I am into the realms of human relationships and ethics. If I *'live and move and have my being'* in God and God lives and moves and has being in me, this announces God Within. There is a divine dimension to all humanity, my and your humanity included. This is universal.

However, because of my ability to participate in decision-making and thus have some control over my behaviour, I do have some control over my response to God Within. My experience of God Within does not obliterate my free will. I can, through my behaviour, return to the universe the benevolence the universe has shown me, or I can refuse to do so.

Jesus is the story of what God Within is all about, what God Within looks like when continuously exposed, uncovered from within humanity, by conscious human decision. When I think of God Within I immediately think of what Jesus said and did, of how he lived, loved and died and of how he continues to be alive for me and many others.

God Between

I have the human experience of God Between, the experience of God between me and others.

When God Within is expressed by one person interacting with another person, then a relationship of love, concern, compassion is created. Love is given and received.

So in the wider community, when justice is done, when reconciliation is achieved, when good laws are passed, when diplomacy triumphs over hostility, when the hungry are fed, when the handicapped are noticed, when corruption is replaced with honesty … I believe God Between is evident and experienced.

When this happens between people, it is, for me, an expression of the human experience of God Between.

With these beliefs I have a reverence for all life engendered in me: a wonderment at the cosmos, a positive attitude to my fellow humans, a challenge to love and live life the way it was meant to be loved and lived. This means I have made a 'faithful rejection' of many of my previous belief emphases and joyfully accepted new ones.

I wish in no way to suggest that others need to have the same beliefs as me. All I am saying is that this works for me at present.

So my present Trinitarian faith statement goes something like this:

I experience God Beyond as a totally limitless inherent mystery in all.

I experience God Within as a totally personally present and continuously inherent mystery in me.

I experience God Between as a totally and continuously involved inherent mystery between people.

The away, theistic, almighty Creator/God has been replaced with an awesome inherent presence, a divine dimension to and in everything: God Beyond.

The godliness within every person which prompts love and compassion of humanity for humanity, is the God dimension of every human being: God Within. Jesus is the total expression of cooperation with, and the uncovering of, God Within.

The godliness being active in human relationships giving my relationships with others an added sacredness, is the God dimension in human love relationships: God Between.

I now have a set of beliefs that I can joyfully embrace, that make sense to me and challenge me to live abundantly.

(Tune: 'Ar hyd y nos'/'All through the night')

Time and space are both a mystery,
God is beyond.
Limitless yet with a history,
God is beyond.
When we think of human millions,
study galaxies in billions,
when we ponder stars in trillions,
God is beyond.

When we use our wealth for sharing,
God is within.
When we live our lives in caring,
God is within.

In our coming and our going,
as we struggle in our growing,
in our learning and our knowing,
God is within.

When we learn to live together,
God is between.
Harmonising with each other,
God is between.
When corruption is deemed loathsome,
when our differences are welcome,
when community is wholesome,
God is between.

George Stuart

A blessing for Trinity Sunday

May the eyes of the seeing Father watch over us
and keep us and ours ever in his gaze.

May the arms of the loving Saviour hold us close
and surround each moment of our lives with his care.

May the wings of the living Spirit shelter each of us
and enfold all our days and our nights with God's peace.
Amen

Simon Taylor

Post-Pentecost lectionary readings

When Sarah laughed and danced

(Genesis 18:1–15, 21:8–10)

When Great Uncle Abram told us that his god had instructed him to leave Haran and to travel to who knows where, we were appalled. The wilderness 'out there' was a dangerous place, and nobody in their right mind spent more time than necessary travelling through it. However, as they say, there is safety in numbers, and numbers were what Father Abram had: kinfolk, servants, flocks and herds, and his wife, Sarai.

I, Joel, was fifteen at the time, and not at all trusting in this invisible god. And so I took along one of our house gods, tucked in my saddlebag with my other belongings.

Over the next 25 years, we travelled back and forth across the desert, down to Egypt and up again, battling with kings and dealing with the day-to-day care of animals and people. Oh yes, life was an adventure.

And all the while Abram would rise early and pray to his invisible god, sometimes even building an altar to him. I, meanwhile, took mine out at night and prayed for the kind of things a young man prays for – wealth, a good wife, lots of sons. I did find a wife and had three sons, as well as two daughters, so life was full and I could thank my god for it. Father Abram, on the other hand, had no son and heir.

So much for his god.

Then one day Abram announced that his god had told him that his name was now to be changed to Abraham, and Sarai was to be called Sarah.

It seemed that I was a sort of favourite of Father Abram, and could talk with him reasonably freely, so after this announcement I asked him why his god had told him to change their names. He said that his god had promised him that he would have offspring *'as numerous as the grains of sand of the earth and the stars in the sky'*, and that their new names reflected that fruitfulness. I almost laughed out loud, but stopped myself in time. It would have been most disrespectful. What a ridiculous idea! He and Great Aunt Sarah were in their nineties at the time, and Sarah was barren. He had one son, Ishmael, by Sarah's maid, Hagar, but no true heir to his or Sarah's name.

Now I was absolutely sure that his god wasn't a patch on mine.

We finally settled by the Oaks of Mamre; and it was there that a peculiar incident occurred. It was mid-afternoon and I was on my way to Father Abraham's tent to ask his advice about something, when these three men appeared. There were no beasts of burden in sight, so they must have walked, but I hadn't seen them coming. They had a quiet authority about them, and when Father Abraham came out of his tent he bowed low to the ground to greet them. He then offered them the traditional hospitality of food and of washing their feet. I was sent to instruct the servants to choose a fat calf to prepare for the feast. Sarah and her maidservants, meanwhile, set about baking cakes to set before them.

While Father Abraham and the men conversed, I noticed Sarah behind the tent opening eavesdropping. Typical nosey woman, I thought, always wanting to know what's going on. But then I realised that I myself was hanging around in the background to do just that.

Then one of the men said, 'Where is your wife Sarah?'

'In the tent,' Abraham replied.

And then came this crazy prediction: 'I will surely return to you in due season, and your wife Sarah shall have a son.'

And Sarah did what I was too polite to do – she laughed.

The man said, 'Why did Sarah laugh, and say, "Shall I indeed bear a child, now that I am old?" Is anything too wonderful for the Lord? I will return to you, in due season, and Sarah shall have a son.'

Sarah denied that she had laughed; and he said, 'Oh yes, you *did* laugh.' But it was just a gentle reproof, as though he wanted to calm her fear.

At that point I left them for my own tent, but kept an eye on them from a distance. The three men eventually left, walking out towards Sodom. But then they just seemed to disappear. Mind you, it could have been a trick of the evening light. Father Abraham stayed where he was, praying to his god, pleading with him about something. I wondered whether this invisible god who made such extravagant promises was listening; and that night took my god out of my bag and thanked him that he wasn't like that. With him I was safe, never having to deal with such nonsense.

It was some time later that I had to eat my words. Sarah announced that she was pregnant. The women in the camp threw a party like nothing you have ever seen – there was feasting, music, singing and dancing around the fire well into the night.

All my certainties about my god were being eroded. I crept up beside Father Abraham, my head burning with questions.

'Father Abraham, how could you have trusted your god to be with you on your journey away from Haran? I carry mine around, so I know he's with me. Yours is invisible.'

He said: 'Joel, my God doesn't belong to me, I belong to him. I don't carry *him* around, *he* carries me. He is not a safe God, but he is faithful.'

'But how do you know, I mean *really* know, it's him talking to you?'

'Sometimes, when things looked bleak, I had my doubts, but I kept praying. And then something would happen, and I'd know that he'd never let me down, even if I didn't understand what he was doing.'

'Something like what?'

Father Abraham gazed into the firelight, and at Sarah, laughing and dancing with the other women, and said quietly, 'Something like this.'

I went back to my tent and to my god and thought hard about what Father Abraham said. A few days later, on a foray into the desert, I 'lost' my little god, leaving it to be buried in the sand whipped up by fierce desert storms.

And then I began to rise early to be with Father Abraham and to learn to pray to this invisible, all-present God, and, to my surprise, heard him speaking to me.

Great Aunt Sarah did have her baby, whom they appropriately named Isaac, 'he who laughs', and I had the privilege of holding him soon after he was born. And all our laughter joined with Isaac's to become the laughter of deep thanksgiving and joy.

Sr Sandra Sears, CSBC

A king or a queen?
(I Samuel 8:4–11, 16–20)

Andy enters waving a Union Jack, singing 'God save the Queen' or 'Land of hope and glory'.

Andy: 'God, save our gracious Queen, long live our noble – ' Oh, hi there, Ada. Isn't it wonderful? I have just been to see the Queen.

Ada: Was it a concert you were at to hear some kind of tribute band?

Andy: No, I went to London to see the real Queen and to join the party for her Diamond Jubilee.

Ada: Did she talk to you? Did you get cucumber sandwiches or tea, or were you drinking champagne?

Andy: Eh … no. But she did wave to me!

Ada: Wave to you? I thought you were at her party; nobody waves to you at a party unless they want to dance with you. Did you dance with the Queen then?

Andy: Eh … no. I did not get to dance with the Queen at Buckingham Palace. I was outside in the crowds when she waved from the balcony – and the crowds went wild and we all waved back to her.

Ada: So you never actually met the Queen, you were just one of the thousands standing outside waving a flag?

Andy: Ehm … yes!

Ada: So, you went all the way to London to a party that you were never invited to, to see someone who had not asked you to come?

Andy: Oh, Ada, when you put it like that it sounds so hollow and empty – but the atmosphere was amazing, wonderful and awesome. She is the head of our country after all.

Ada: Now, Andy. Did you not tell me once that God was the King and head of our church and country?

Andy: Ehm ... I might have said that.

Ada: So if God is King and head of our country and the church why do we need someone else to fulfil that roll?

Andy: Now, Ada. Every country needs a king or queen.

Ada: But America does not have a king, they have a president.

Andy: Yes, but ...

Ada: And Australia is a republic: they don't have a king or queen either.

Andy: Well ...

Ada: And China doesn't believe in kings or queens either; they even did away with all their emperors.

Andy: Okay, I get your point, Ada: not every country has a king or a queen.

Ada: The Bible tells us that Israel wanted a king so they could be like every other nation, and God did not like the idea very much. He told them that they didn't need a king, that they were special and holy people, and that God was to be their King and leader.

Andy: I remember that.

Ada: God told Samuel that if they got a king like all the other nations they would end up sending their sons and daughters to war. They would become captive to the king's mood swings, and would get distracted from following God.

Andy: Aye, the people thought that the king would fight their battles for them, but it would turn out that *they* were fighting the king's battles.

Ada: But the people were persistent; they thought that they knew best. They did not want to be different from other nations and so they insisted that a king would be a great idea, even though God warned them against going down that route.

Andy: Maybe we cannot blame the king or the queen for all the faults of the nation. Maybe the people have to take some responsibility for the bad choices they have made over the years.

Ada: Aye, and maybe it is a timely reminder to all of us that God is our real King and the one we must all answer to!

John Murning, Spill the Beans

We really want a king

(I Samuel 8:4–11, 16–20)

The people said to Samuel,
'We really want a king!
Please find someone to lead us,
to fight for us and win!'

Samuel told the people,
'Here's what a king will do:
he'll send your sons to battle,
he'll make life hard for you!

'The best of everything you have
the king will make his own!
You'll have to work much harder,
and then you'll moan and groan!'

But the people said to Samuel,
'We want a king to reign,
like all the other countries!
We want to be the same!'

Samuel told the people,
'But we've got God above,
who only wants the best for us,
and leads and rules with love!'

But the people wouldn't listen.
'We want a king!' they said.
'What will I do, Lord?' Samuel cried.
God answered, 'Go ahead,

give them what they ask for,
a king to rule them all.'
So Samuel searched the land
and chose a man called Saul.

What kind of king, I wonder,
did Saul turn out to be?
Did he make the people happy?
We'll have to wait and see.

Jo Love, Spill the Beans

David is chosen to be king
(I Samuel 15:34–16:13)

Have you ever done something that felt like a really good idea, but turned out to be a horrible mistake?

Remember the story about the people wanting a king? Samuel thought it was a bad idea. God thought it was a bad idea. But all the people thought it was a good idea. They wanted a king – they really wanted a king!

So finally God said, 'OK then.' And Samuel said, 'Here he is then. King Saul.'

Did everyone live happily ever after?

Oh no! Oh dear!

Saul wasn't very good at being a king. And God wished he had never made Saul the king!

So did God say, 'That's it! No more kings! They're a bad idea!'?

Did God say, 'I told you so!'?

Did God say, 'I knew this would happen!'?

Did God say, 'Well, didn't I warn you?!'?

Did God say, 'See what happens when you don't listen!'?

No, he didn't. God is kinder and more patient than that. He knew the people still wanted to have a king, even though it might not be the best idea. So God tried again. He asked Samuel to find a new king. This time it was a boy called David. He was the youngest in his family and he was very good at looking after sheep.

What on earth made God think a young shepherd boy could be king? But that's who he chose. David.

What kind of king, I wonder, did David turn out to be?

Did he make the people happy?

We'll have to wait and see.

Jo Love, Spill the Beans

Wee Davy

(1 Samuel 17:32–49)

Andy is trying to put on some clothes that obviously no longer fit him, when Ada comes wandering in. Andy is singing the Beatles' song 'Yesterday'.

Ada: Andy, what are you doing?

Andy: I'm checking out some of my old wardrobe, the clothes I used to wear to the disco, when I was in my prime.

Ada: Andy, you have put on about three stone since those days, none of those clothes will ever fit you.

Andy: Ada, you can be awfy hurtful at times. I was just getting a wee bit nostalgic and remembering what life used to be like, and thought about checking out my old gear. Do you no' remember getting dressed up when you were a wee girl?

Ada: Aye, I remember. I loved dressing up. Sometimes I would pretend to be a little princess, and I would put on my dress and tiara. Sometimes I would put on my mum's clothes and pretend to be her. And sometimes I would put on my big sister's make-up and pretend to be a famous pop star.

Andy: Do you know, I used to dress up in my Superman outfit, and I refused to take it off because I thought I would lose my superpowers. And then there was my goalkeeping shirt that I wore, and I used to pretend that I was Lev Yashin the famous Russian goalie.

Ada: And guess what, Andy, people still dress up today to try and be something they are not. Teachers are sometimes told to get dressed up in a suit if they have to look very professional or if they have a meeting with a difficult parent. They call that power-dressing.

Andy: Aye, and the wains at the school can tell who the cool kids are, or who the geeks are, and whether someone is a mosher or a goth or a nerd by what they wear.

Ada: And was it not Mark Twain who once said that 'clothes make the man. Naked people have little or no influence on society.'

Andy: Ooooh, where did you get that from?

Ada: Well, I was thinking about our Bible story today. There was wee Davy, trying to put on the king's suit of armour to keep him safe, and he ended up just looking ridiculous. He couldn't walk, he couldn't see because of a great big muckle helmet, and the sword the king gave him was far too big to even lift off the ground.

Andy: Aye, he was putting on that heavy metal suit to represent Israel in the battle with the Philistines.

Ada: The Israelites were apparently all feart of these Philistines because they were like giants, and especially their champion called Goliath. He was massive.

Andy: But didn't wee Davy say he was willing to fight, and everybody laughed at the thought of a wee laddie going up against a giant? But Davy wasn't thinking about what might happen to him. He believed that God was on his side, and if God was on his side then anything was possible.

Ada: Aye, yer right, Andy. Big Goliath was laughing at Israel and their God too, but wee Davy was not feart of anything. He just wanted to be himself, and fight the only way he knew, with his stick and his sling.

Andy: It's funny how we think that we need all sorts of wonderful tools or gifts and talents to serve God, when all that we really need is ourselves.

Ada: Aye, wee Davy just put his faith and trust in God and went for it, believing that God would help him.

Andy: So we really don't need to get dressed up in our Sunday best to come to church. All that God wants is for us to be ourselves and trust in him.

Ada: That's the idea. And when we put our trust in God even unbeatable giants can be defeated, as wee Davy proved.

John Murning, Spill the Beans

Deep within

(Mark 5:25–34)

Deep within I bleed.
I have bled for twelve years.
Poked and probed to no avail,
no more shall a healer touch me.

Deep within I hurt,
emotional not physical pain,
the pain of being put aside by my husband,
the pain of being called unclean by my community.

Deep within I long to touch this healer,
just the tassel of his cloak,
secretly so he won't be polluted …
if I but reach out my hand.

Deep within power has gone.
Who touched me?

As I turn I know
that someone has come to me.

Deep within me you dwell.
Deep within you I dwell.
Deep sounds to deep
and I am healed.

Angie Allport

Blessed

(Matthew 5:1–12)

Blessed are the vulnerable,
for they know
the street map of God's grace;

blessed are those who mingle
their tears with those of God,
for they will hold hands
with the broken-hearted;

blessed are the humble,
for they open their arms
to those tossed aside by us;

blessed are those who walk
side by side with the bullied,
for they offer God's hope
to those who have seen theirs
crushed into the playground dirt;

blessed are those whose hearts
are empty of ego and fears,
for they shall be filled
with compassion for all;

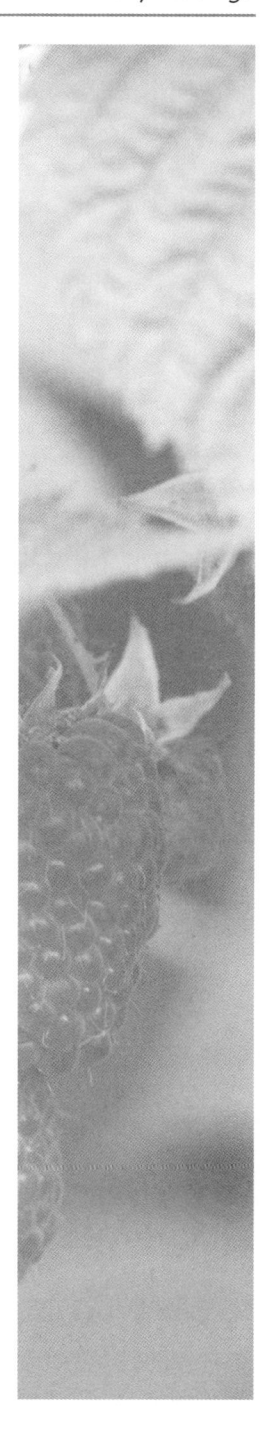

blessed are those who build bridges
using the bricks the fearful
would use to build walls,
for they shall dance
with their sisters and brothers;

blessed are those who are accused
of welcoming the outsiders,
of standing with trans kids,
of seeking justice for everyone,
for they open their hearts freely;

blessed are you
when you simply live as God's beloved:
always being just,
always sharing kindness,
always walking with God.

Thom M Shuman

The sparrows' story

(Matthew 10:26–30)

Somewhere on a high branch on a spring day in Galilee.

Sparrow 1: Did you hear him?

Sparrow 2: Yes, I heard him.

Sparrow 1: He tells amazing stories, doesn't he?

Sparrow 2: Did you hear the one about the party that no one would go to?

Sparrow 1: Yes, and the one about the coins that the woman lost.

Sparrow 2: And did you see him talking to that man hiding in the sycamore tree?

Sparrow 1: Yes – what a strange place for a human to perch!

Sparrow 2: They do odd things, don't they, these humans?

Sparrow 1: But he seems to love them all the same. Do you remember when he and his friends were walking through the cornfields?

Sparrow 2: Yes, it was on the Sabbath and they were really hungry.

Sparrow 1: And they picked some seed-heads and ate them.

Sparrow 2: It's strange that they like the same food as us.

Sparrow 1: And do you remember that picnic with all those people?

Sparrow 2: I was so full I could hardly move.

Sparrow 1: All those breadcrumbs!

Sparrow 2: And those flakes of fish – they were so tasty …

Sparrow 1: I wish he'd do that again.

Sparrow 2: Me too – it was soooo good.

Sparrow 1: But this morning, did you hear him?

Sparrow 2: I certainly heard him.

Sparrow 1: He talked about us.

Sparrow 2: Us, us two sparrows.

Sparrow 1: He's mentioned birds before and we were chuffed about that.

Sparrow 2: But this morning he talked about us sparrows.

Sparrow 1: To be fair we've had a mention before.

Sparrow 2: A mention from King David.

Sparrow 1: Us and the swallows making nests.

Sparrow 2: Nests in the temple.

Sparrow 1: But it's the first time we've had a mention from Jesus.

Sparrow 2: Two sparrows who could be sold for a penny – that's definitely us.

Sparrow 1: What did he say again?

Sparrow 2: He said that God cares about us.

Sparrow 1: Yes, and he said that God is concerned about what happens to us.

Sparrow 2: That God knows who we are.

Sparrow 1: And he said that nothing will be secret.

Sparrow 2: No more hiding in sycamore trees.

Sparrow 1: Even sparrows can tell their story.

Sparrow 2: Tell each other how much we are cared about and loved.

Sparrow 1: And do you remember what he said about humans?

Sparrow 2: He said every hair on their heads God knew about and had counted.

Sparrow 1: Seems a bit unfair on the babies and the older baldy ones!

Sparrow 2: Yes, I thought that as well.

Sparrow 1: I think feathers are better.

Sparrow 2: Much, much warmer.

Sparrow 1: David said we can shelter under God's feathers.

Sparrow 2: Safe, like a chick, under its mother's wings.

Sparrow 1: I'm glad we heard Jesus talking this morning.

Sparrow 2: Talking about us sparrows.

Sparrow 1: Do you think the humans understand what he's telling them?

Sparrow 2: Do they know how much they are cared about and loved?

Sparrow 1: They need to tell each other their stories.

Sparrow 2: Encourage each other to keep listening to what Jesus says.

Sparrow 1: I'm getting hungry – it must be time for dinner.

Sparrow 2: Me too, my beak is definitely twitching.

Sparrow 1: Do you think any of these people have dropped any bread crumbs?

Sparrow 2: Let's fly around and see what we can find.

Ruth Burgess, Spill the Beans

Spurgie

(Matthew 10:26–30)

Good morning.

I hope you're good at guessing.

I want to play – 'What am I?'

You ready?

Right – I'm small.

I sometimes live in trees.

I usually live near people.

I've got feathers.

My feathers are brown and white and black.

My name begins with S.

Yes, you've got me – I'm a sparrow.

And because I live in Scotland I'm sometimes called Spurgie. I've got a cousin in the north of England and he's called Spuggy, and a friend in Yorkshire and she's called Spadger.

I want to tell you a story today about two sparrows who lived a long time ago in Galilee. You might have heard of Galilee; there's a big lake there called the Sea of Galilee, and it's where Jesus lived and went about talking to people and telling stories.

Now these two sparrows, like all of us sparrows, lived near to people, because we sparrows know that where there's people, there's food. We'll eat most things. We like seeds and corn best, but we'll eat breadcrumbs and cake crumbs as well. And human beings are so untidy – and they often drop bits of food, especially when they're eating sandwiches outdoors, so we stay close to them and we eat up all the crumbs that they drop on the ground.

These two sparrows had noticed how many people came together to listen to Jesus when he was telling stories, and they often found a tree to perch in and they listened too. They noticed that Jesus often mentioned animals in his stories. There was a story about a man who looked after pigs, and another one about a man who lost one of his sheep. Once these two sparrows had been near to Jesus when Jesus was talking to thousands of people. And there had been a huge picnic and there were breadcrumbs everywhere and flakes of fish too. The sparrows had had a great feast that day – they were so full they could hardly fly.

One day when the sparrows were listening to Jesus they heard him say that God cared about everyone and that God was always interested to know what people did and what happened to them. And then they had a big surprise – they heard Jesus say that God cared about sparrows. They were really pleased about that. They had heard Jesus talking about how people were important to God before, but now Jesus had said that sparrows were important too. They were chuffed! Jesus must have noticed them listening and they'd become part of his story.

And they went about telling all the other sparrows what they'd heard: God cares about sparrows. God cares what happens to sparrows. Sparrows are important to God.

And those sparrows who were told about God's love for them, told their chicks what Jesus had said, and their chicks told their chicks, all down the years. And my granddad told my mother, and my mother told me. And I know that God cares about me. And that I can tell every sparrow I meet that Jesus cares about them too.

So, remember my name?

I'm Spurgie and my cousin in Newcastle is called Spuggy and my friend in Yorkshire is called Spadger. You might see me and my friends in your garden or in a tree in your playground. We might be talking about God; we might be telling each other that we're hungry.

Do you remember what we like to eat? Seeds and corn and breadcrumbs and cake crumbs.

And we will be very very happy if you give us some food.

Ruth Burgess, Spill the Beans

A cup of cold water

(Matthew 10:40–42)

A short monologue to follow the Bible reading, beginning in a slightly disparaging tone and becoming increasingly serious and reflective. The reader pours a cup of cold water from a jug before speaking, and holds the cup as they speak.

A cup of cold water. Would you really call this a welcoming thing to offer? Good hospitality? Just plain cold water from the tap? Not very impressive. Not to me or you anyway. Just turn on the tap and here it is, without any effort. Just boring old water. What a scoosh, if you don't mind me saying. Colourless, pretty tasteless, but on the plus side, it's clean and fresh, safe and reliable.

Pause and drink.

A cup of cold water to drink. It's the least you can do for someone. The very least. The bare minimum in fact. Even if you run out of tea and coffee and haven't so much as a digestive biscuit in the house, you can surely give a cup of water.

Pause and drink.

A cup of cold water. One in six people can only dream of this. A billion people across the world would give anything to be able to turn on a tap and pour out a cup of cold water. Every year, millions of people, millions of ordinary people just like us, die from preventable diseases linked directly to the lack of safe water.

Pause and drink.

A cup of cold water. It can mean so little. It can mean so much. Either way, thirst-quenching matters. It's kingdom work.

Pause and drink.

Cheers!

Jo Love, Spill the Beans

A special welcome
(Matthew 10:40–42)

Stephen wanted to do something special to welcome his uncles. He hadn't seen them for a long time. Uncle Mick and Uncle Gerry and their bouncing poodle Alfie would be travelling all day to get from their house to Stephen's by teatime. They were coming to visit for a week's holiday.

Dad and Mum had been busy all day, tidying the house, and even making sure the garden looked its best. Stephen went into the kitchen, the sitting room, the bathroom, the bedroom, and outside into the garden, looking for something he could do to give the best welcome. But it looked like Mum and Dad had thought of everything.

The grass was cut. There was a bunch of balloons tied to the gate! The front door sat open in the afternoon sun, and the hallway was swept. There was a lovely smell of a cake baking in the oven. The teapot and cups were on the table. There were clean towels by the shower and a vase of flowers in the spare room. Was there anything more to do?

Stephen was so excited as he thought about seeing Uncle Mick and Uncle Gerry again, but he wished he could do something special for their arrival.

'Here they are!' called Dad suddenly from the garden, and Stephen heard his Mum's footsteps, so he ran outside after her to see his uncles and his parents all hugging and saying hello, with Alfie bouncing around on the grass.

'Come on in!' said Mum, and soon they were all sitting round the kitchen table with cups of tea and chocolate cake.

'What a welcome!' laughed Uncle Gerry.

'You always make us feel at home!' cried Uncle Mick.

They were so busy chatting, that no one noticed as Stephen went to the cupboard by the sink, filled a plastic bowl with water, and put it on the floor. Alfie's tail was wagging even faster than usual as he lapped up a long drink.

'Oh Stephen, thank you! What a lovely thing to do!' said Uncle Mick.

'You thought about welcoming Alfie too!' said Uncle Gerry.

And they hugged their favourite nephew, who always did such special things.

Jo Love, Spill the Beans

The sower went forth to sow
(Matthew 13:1–9,18–23)

When I signed up for the job, I was given a parcel of land to work. Now, I wasn't exactly a farmer, but what I lacked in knowledge I made up for in enthusiasm – or at least that's how I figured it. I read everything I could on the subject. Then it was time for the practical stuff.

Firstly, I went into town for supplies and introduced myself to the locals. I soon found out what they thought of my acreage. One old codger said, 'You must be joking! Even the wallabies there have to pack a cut lunch!' After the laughter had died down I told them that really it was the Master who chose it for me, and they laughed even harder. 'More fool you!' was their response. I tried to explain my relationship with my Master (how I longed for them to get to know him!), but it was no use. So I knew that each time I went into town I'd be in for some good-natured ribbing.

However, it wasn't long before I found out that they were right – at least about the land, which wasn't what you might call 'fertile'. In fact it was mainly rocks, with a few patches of reasonable soil between them. However, I didn't let that daunt me. I duly went out and scattered the seed willy-nilly across the landscape, rocks and all. Suffice it to say, the yield wasn't what you might call 'abundant'.

To supplement my income, I ran a few sheep and goats, but even that wasn't very profitable. Grass for grazing wasn't in good supply. But despite the old bloke's predictions, the local inhabitants – kangaroo, wallaby, wombats – seemed to manage, except in drought conditions, when I took pity on them and fed them.

I still persisted, season after season; but eventually I became despondent, and went to the Master to find out what I was doing wrong. We would meet regularly on top of the hill at the back of the house, where there was a large, flat rock. There I would sit and we'd talk.

As I said, I was depressed, and not a little angry. After all, it was he who had allotted me this uncompromising bit of scrub, so what did he expect? Grain trucks lined up to collect the crops? Fatted lambs being carted off to market? I spent time swinging between blaming me and blaming him. He said nothing.

Eventually I lapsed into morose silence (two could play at this game) and picked idly at a bit of greenery next to where I was sitting. Suddenly I realised that it shouldn't really be there. This was, after all, solid rock. But there it was. One of the seeds had obviously fallen into a deep groove where a little soil had accumulated, and by some miracle survived to struggle up to the light.

My Master broke the silence. He simply said, 'You know, a single tiny seed can split rocks like this one … eventually.'

That was all he said, but it set me thinking. I had resented the lack of evidence of my toil, but it was there nevertheless. In fact it was right under my nose. I thought of my neighbours who viewed my work as irrelevant, or worse, scorned my Master and his choice of land. But somehow the sight of that lone seedling made it all worthwhile. I didn't need their approval. There were more important things going on here than planting abundant crops or raising fat, sturdy lambs.

I don't know what the outcome of my work will be, but maybe, just maybe, the seeds that I sow might find root in the hearts and minds of my neighbours, and grow enough to split their crusty, defensive shells and allow a bit of sunlight in. They might even get to know the Master … eventually.

Either way, my job is to sow. The rest is up to him.

Sr Sandra Sears, CSBC

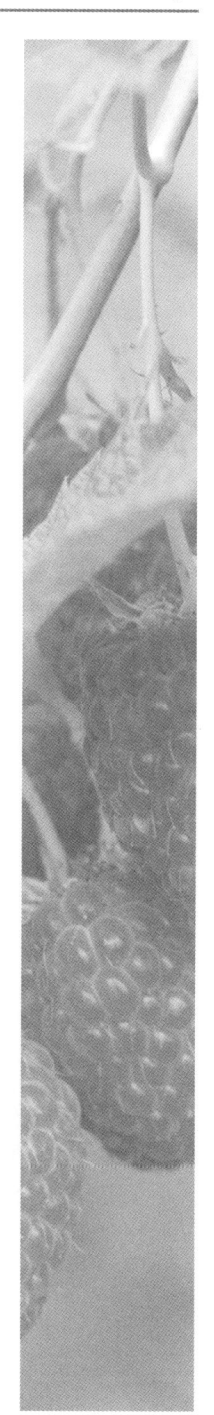

Gardeners and bonfires

(Matthew 13:24–30, 36–43)

Andy: Hey, Ada. I think Jesus must have been a good gardener.

Ada: What makes you say that, Andy?

Andy: Well, he is always talking about seeds and plants and growing things.

Ada: Aye, he certainly does, Andy.

Andy: Maybe they could invite him on to *Gardeners' Question Time*.

Ada: I think that Jesus is more interested in people than plants though, Andy. He only uses these horticultural illustrations to make a point about people or the Kingdom of God.

Andy: Aye, but, Ada, he does talk about the weeds getting in among the good plants in the Bible today.

Ada: He does, Andy, but he is talking about the communities where we all live.

Andy: But, Ada, we live in a tenement building where there are not many gardens!

Ada: Aye, Andy, I know that, but I think Jesus is saying that in every community there are good people trying to do his work and others who just couldn't care less, and even some who are very against his work.

Andy: So who are these good people?

Ada: Jesus says it is those people who do the things God asks of them, like fight for justice and care for the poor, the needy and the vulnerable. The people who show love and compassion and practise forgiveness toward others.

Andy: Like you and the minister do, Ada?

Ada: Well, I try my best, Andy. You do too, sometimes.

Andy: So who are the bad guys, the weeds in our community?

Ada: Well, perhaps they are the people who undermine a sense of community. The drug pushers on the street corners, those who beat up their wives and weans, those loan sharks who bleed people dry of their hard-earned cash. These are just some of the weeds I can see in _____! *(your city/town).*

Andy: So why does God not just zap these baddies and burn them up like a pile of weeds on a bonfire?

Ada: Maybe he is giving them a chance to reform. After all, a weed is still a plant and that has some value, Andy. Maybe it is not up to us to judge and condemn. That's up to God to decide their fate.

Andy: Well, if it was left to me, I know what I would do!

Ada: Yes, we know what you would like to do to them, but that is not your call, Andy. You are challenged to continue growing to your own full potential in the sight of God.

Andy: Aye, but guess what?

Ada: What, Andy?

Andy: There is a big bad burny fire for those who remain as weeds, it says here, and there will be weeping there and gnashing of teeth!

Ada: Well, Andy, you better go and put your dentures in just in case!

John Murning, Spill the Beans

Noah's big picnic

(John 6:1–14)

For Dawod, who told us with such authority that the little boy who gave Jesus the loaves and fish was called Noah.

Mother: Hello, Noah. Did you have a good time?

Noah: Oh yes, Mum! The best ever – it was wicked!

Mother: That's good. Did you eat all your picnic?

Noah: No, I ……

Mother: Oh, Noah, don't tell me you fed it to the seagulls! Your Dad was up very early to catch fish for us, and your Gran made those barley loaves especially for you because she knows you like them.

Noah: No, honestly, I didn't feed it to the seagulls – I shared it with everybody.

Mother: Oh, you mean Reuben and Samuel and Levi?

Noah: No! Everybody! Everybody there! The whole crowd – more than five thousand people!

Mother: Now, come on, Noah! What have I told you about telling fibs and making up all sorts of nonsense?

Noah: But, Mum, I'm not making things up! There were more than five thousand people there and they all ate my bread and fish!

Mother: Oh, Noah, don't be ridiculous! How could you possibly have shared five little barley loaves and two fish with that many people?

Noah: Well, I didn't ……

Mother: You see, I knew you were telling fibs!

Noah: No, Mum, you don't understand! It wasn't me – I didn't make the food go round five thousand people – it was Jesus! He'd spent the afternoon telling stories and teaching us how, if we love God, we should help others.

Then it started getting late and the disciples came round, asking if anybody had any food to share. Some people pretended they hadn't, but I gave them the picnic you gave me. They took it to Jesus, and he said a prayer – and then suddenly there was enough food for everyone! In fact, they even gathered up twelve baskets of leftovers! Oh, Mum, you should have been there – it was awesome! When I grow up, I want to be just like Jesus.

Mother: Well, son, it sounds to me like you've already started if you were prepared to share what you had with other people. I'm proud of you, Noah, I really am!

Janet Pybon

Father's Day

Like a father to us

We thank you, Lord, that you are like a father to us:
you provide us with all we need to live.
We thank you for food and drink,
for home and family:
O God, our Father:
we praise you.

We thank you that you watch over us
and we are always in your loving gaze.
You see what makes us happy and sad;
you are there to help us when we need you:
O God, our Father:
we praise you.

You are kind and forgiving;
you understand us and are patient with us.
When we do what is wrong you forgive us,
and help us to do what is right:
O God, our Father:
we praise you.

Your love for us never ends;
you don't grow tired of us or get fed up with us.
You always find joy in us, your children,
and promise you will never abandon or leave us.
O God, our Father:
we praise you.

We thank you that you care for everything around us,
for our homes and families, our friends and our *village/town/city*.
From the smallest to the tallest and whatever's in between,
you are concerned for everything in this world.
O God, our Father:
we praise you.

We praise you for sending Jesus as our friend,
for he tells us that we can be in your family too.
With you we can know joy and peace

as we discover your perfect love.
O God, our Father:
we praise you. Amen

Simon Taylor

Dads and summer

I have been a gardener for a number of years.
The men I work with do not accept this.
I'm constantly told that I'm not a real gardener
and that my qualifications are not worth
the paper they are written on.

But when I'm pruning roses and passers-by greet me cheerily,
I know why I do the job.

When I'm eager to use the sit-on tractor to cut the grass,
but don't get a chance to due to the 'pecking order',
I happily push the lawnmower
and smell the delicious scent of summer anyway.

There's not always blue skies and sunshine in summer –
and this year has been one of the wettest.
On wet days I feel God is giving me some time off
and I do other things, such as tidy the yard or the greenhouse.

My dad is undergoing chemotherapy for advanced prostate cancer,
and while I'm working I think of funny things to make my dad laugh,
and set him little missions to take his mind off things.

It's funny that I now get my hands dirty for a living,
because I remember being smacked as a child
for having muddy hands.

Now I have to hold my dad's hand
as he takes this journey with God.

Susan Lindsay

Father and son

I am exactly the same age as my father when he died in 1985. There is something poignant and sobering about facing this life marker. I suspect it is reason enough to explain my recent, more than usual, pondering of life with my father – the bitter and sweet, the tough and tender, the shameful and proud.

'My mother told me never to go near the water until I learned how to swim.' That was my father's humorous, yet character-revealing, risk-averse response each time I asked him to go swimming with us in Lake Erie. Or maybe it was wisdom, considering how polluted Lake Erie was at the time. He loved to laugh, tell and hear funny stories and drop in one-liners. As he aged his favourite line was, 'I get stiff in all the wrong places.'

My father covered his pain with humour, loving presence and hard manual work. The woman he dearly loved became chronically ill at my birth. We watched her steady decline, as if sitting on a thin limb which might break at any moment.

As pain and loss consumed her vitality, bent her frame and distorted all her joints, my father tenderly absorbed my mother's rants. He taught me compassionate presence in the face of limitations and frailty.

By most standards, my dad would not have been considered a successful man. An auto mechanic, he never made enough money for us to have our own home until I was in high school. Instead, we lived with grandparents.

Growing up on a farm, he never completed a high-school education. Yet I remember many nights when he schooled me in math (until solid geometry defeated us both). He taught me the fine art of pitching baseballs: throw the ball from your full height and bring the pitch in just above the knees; or swing the ball from a sweeping sidearm that swoops the ball in low across the plate. He was a patient, persistent coach, never yelling and always guiding. We loved each other but rarely displayed physical warmth.

We visited my mother's grave a year after her death, in 1980. We stood quietly together for some time, until he softly said, 'You've noticed that one side of this cemetery is filled with large, ornate tombstones. Your mother and I have markers that are flush with the ground. We chose this side because everyone is equal over here.'

Perhaps my most significant learning came after a scene which still haunts me. I was probably in the ninth grade at the time. The newspaper boy knocked on the door of my grandparents' house to collect for the daily he delivered, a total of $2.35 for the month. I called my father to come. My father rifled through his pockets but found only a small amount of change. He turned to me and asked to borrow the money. I made a very smart-mouthed comment about his need to pay me back, since I had made the money mowing yards. His face showed his pain and I left the room to get the money. He never scolded me. Maybe his shame was even greater than mine. I ached for days about what I'd said.

At some point I made the choice to accept this man just as he was. I didn't need or want him to be more than who, at the core, he was. I look back and thrill with gratitude that I didn't get locked into a struggle to make him someone else. This feels like the completion of love: the acceptance of the other as the person they are. Professionally, I spent a lot of time counselling people who expended enormous energy trying to remake their parents, their spouse, their children, rather than accepting them with their limitations, gifts and graces.

As I cross the threshold of the age at which my father died, I am grateful for the gifts this humble man gave me.

Benjamin Pratt

Let us pray for fathers

Let us pray for fathers:
for loving fathers,
for wise fathers,
for absent fathers,
for cruel fathers,
for fathers who are ill,
for fathers who have died.
God, who Jesus called father,
hear our prayers.

Let us pray for fathers who play with their children,
for fathers who are unable to find work,
for fathers who are carers,
for fathers whose work keeps them away from their children.
God, who Jesus called father,
hear our prayers.

Let us pray for fathers who love their partners,
for fathers whose children are adults,
for fathers whose children care for them,
for fathers who have more than one family.
God, who Jesus called father,
hear our prayers.

Let us pray for those who became parents today,
for our own parents,
for our friends' parents,
for parents who are unable to have children,
for families we know who need our support and prayers.
God, who Jesus called father,
hear our prayers.

Loving God,
as fathers,
as mothers,
as grandparents,
as children,
we ask you to bless us
as we bring you our prayers. **Amen**

Ruth Burgess

A Father's Day blessing

(Based on Psalm 121)

May God our Father keep you in his love,
and be your comfort and your strength.

May God be your hope and support,
your light and your protector.

May the Father, who never ceases to care for us,
watch over your going out and your coming in,
from this time on and for evermore. Amen

Simon Taylor

All creatures
great and small

The animals in the zoo

(Tune: 'All things bright and beautiful')

Praise God for the animals,
the birds and fishes too,
all the wondrous creatures
that live here in the zoo.

From alpacas to zebras,
to dolphins in the sea,
to eagles high above us
God gives them space to be.

Praise God for the animals,
the birds and fishes too,
all the wondrous creatures
that live here in the zoo.

The lions and the llamas,
the leaping kangaroo,
the monkeys and the meerkats
are playing in the zoo.

Praise God for the animals,
the birds and fishes too,
all the wondrous creatures
that live here in the zoo.

When we cut down the forests,
throw plastic waste in seas,
pump poison in the airwaves,
it's death to such as these.

*Praise God for the animals,
the birds and fishes too,
all the wondrous creatures
that live here in the zoo.*

The zoo gives food and shelter,
brings little ones to birth,
provides a home and future
for creatures of the earth.

*Praise God for the animals,
the birds and fishes too,
all the wondrous creatures
that live here in the zoo.*

Jan Berry

Little monsters

Little monsters.
Huge black eyes bulging under sealed lids.
Swollen bellies.
Bare, pink skin.
Garish yellow, gaping beaks.
Magnify them up
and they would be nightmarish aliens.
But in a few weeks
the hand of God will craft these tiny horrors
into beloved garden birds.

Brian Ford

This far north

This far north I had not expected
to be welcomed by larks overhead,
but twice this week I have been enchanted
to see them and to follow where they led.
Across headlands, soft with thyme and heather,
in open skies to distant Orkney isles,
blue in the melting mist, where Orkney weather
changes by the moment and beguiles
our senses, until nothing else can matter,
only your call above and the soft turf
beneath our feet as we move on together
toward the clifftops and the rolling surf.
The larks are calling to us Come, oh come,
where earth and sea and heaven all are one.

Brian Hick

June in the Danube Delta

Waterways through a world of secrets,
a world we cannot enter
of voles and otters, rats and moles;
tall reed banks
whose rush-canes waving high
make the thick screen
reflected in the shaded water;
soft grey-green willow foliage
lightly brush, as to caress
the carp-rich stream.

Broad-winged damselflies
flit like messengers across our bows,
while floating lilies,
yellow or white, catching the sun
make play platforms for glurping toads and frogs.

Catching our eye, a graceful little egret
perches erect and still.
Way above the whispering poplars
high in the summer sky
a pelican army wheels in display formation.

Travelling quiet and slow
in this wetland wilderness
allows our inner peace to grow.

Liz Gregory-Smith

Birdsong

The soothing melody of a bird,
the gentle rustle of the wind,
the hum of bees,
otherwise silence;
the sun sparkling on the sea,
white clouds motionless
over the Paps of Jura.

The stress and turmoil
of the past few weeks
fall away in this distant place,
far away from where I have come.

The bird sings to me
of solace and hope;
and not to me alone,
but to all who hear him
and are open to receive his song.

Katherine Rennie

The trouble with adders

I was looking for my third adder this morning.
Not that the adders are mine in any way.
I don't think they would take too kindly to petting
or to being taken for a walk on a lead.
But I've seen two in recent weeks as they come out
to enjoy the sun in this very different summer.
At my approach they scuttle away, matching my anxiety
with theirs. I wish they would stay longer so that
I could better appreciate the tattoos on their back.
The paths that were lined with orchids in May
are now pancaked by wandering cattle.
Insects hassle from the high bracken.
Heat hovers over everything. Mud is just a memory.
I kept looking for the not my adder and
was sorry that he or she did not show up.
Perhaps there was adderly business to attend to.
The trouble with looking for adders is that you miss looking up.
Too often my eyes are grounded. I need to look up more often.

John Randall

Goats don't do metanoia

Many Sundays I drive
out along a lovely ridge
with beautiful vistas
of rolling hills, tiny farms.
It is an effort to remember
that over one rise topped
by an eighteenth-century house,
inhabited but crumbling,
the farmer keeps livestock,
including goats that loiter
on the country road.
Like sheep, goats are
not very intelligent,
will stand in the lane,
stare down a preacher
in a battered old car
who is a little late for liturgy,
and slightly afraid of goats
who butt when confronted
at close quarters by clergy.
They remind me of parables,
become fodder for sermons
when, in their recalcitrance,
they remain sternly immobile.
According to the story,
God places them firmly
on the divine left hand,
does not, I hope, consign
them to eternal fire prepared
for Satan's minions,
but not for us, who are also
stupid, stubborn creatures.

Bonnie Thurston

The wasps and the midges

Whizzing down country lanes,
puffing up steep hills.
A gentle bend here,
a sharp turn there.
Wasps out in force,
so are the midges.

Stopping for rest,
taking out picnic,
jeely pieces,
can of Irn Bru.
Wasps out in force,
so are the midges

Looking around,
blue sky,
green grass,
wild flowers.
Wasps out in force,
so are the midges

All things bright and beautiful,
All creatures great and small,
All things wise and wonderful,
The Lord God made them all.

The wasps out in force.
So are the midges.

Why, God, did you make
the wasps and the midges?!

Mary Whittaker

Summer in July

For warm seaside days

For beaches and kites.
For rock-pools and shells.
For surfboards and waves.
For buckets and spades.
For warm seaside days.
Praise!

Avis Palmer

Summer in Skye

I read about the poet who is addicted to this island –
to its power, its magic, its beauty.
He asks how you find the heart of an island.
He says you begin by not looking for it at all.
I am searching, looking for a path of my own.
I watch and wait; I walk and explore,
for I too am addicted, pulled,
drawn by the mystique of the being greater than myself,
bigger and deeper than any of us.

I explore the coastline, walk the paths,
sit, rock-like, waiting for the otter to crack open its crab.

If I don't look too hard,
maybe I'll see the light glimmering on the waves,
feel the breath stirring in the rushes,
feel the peace in the misty uncertainty,
the freshness in the fine drizzle.

The poet looks for the heart of the island.
I watch and wait, looking and yet not looking.

Judy Dinnen

Summer season

I love the lazy days of summer,
idling, strolling in the heat,
looking for the coolness of shade,
eating outdoors, picnics and barbecues,
swimming in cool sea or pool,
relaxing with friends over a glass of wine,
letting pressure and stress drop away.

But summer can be lonely:
long days stretching into empty evenings.
No busy routine to fill the hours,
friends away sending Facebook images
of distant exotic travels.

God, in the ever-circling seasons,
be with me in the delights of summer,
and keep me company through the long empty days.

Jan Berry

The sun is shining

The sun is shining.
It wraps us up
like a boiling kettle.

The sun is gold.
I feel it bright.

And the bats are scared
that their hearts
will burn.

Ian (aged 7)

The Alpha and the Omega

'I am Alpha and Omega, the beginning and the end, the first and the last.'

Revelation 22:13 (KJV)

God is our refuge and strength, a very present help in trouble.
Therefore will not we fear, though the earth be removed,
and though the mountains be carried into the midst of the sea;
though the waters ... roar and be troubled, though the mountains shake ...

Psalm 46:1–3 (KJV)

(Tune: 'Sursum corda')

You are the start of time; you are the end.
And so, in faith, we seek to comprehend
how you might dwell with us, eternally;
how broad, how deep, how sure your love can be.

You are the Alpha; from the first of days,
you offered Light to lead us in your ways;
you caused the sun to set, the dawn to break;
you willed the seas to shift, the hills to shake.

You are the Omega; your love will last,
when even time itself, and life, are past.
You set the stars for night, the moon to trace
a pathway through the vastness of your space.

You make the seasons change, you feed the land;
you give your Word, so we might understand.
Your faithful hand is found in everything,
in life, in death, in all creation brings.

You are the summer flowers, the seeds that grow;
you are the rain that falls, the winds that blow;
you are the glassy sea, the storms that rage;
you are our constancy for every age.

You were the start and you will be the end,
and so, our thanks from earth to heaven ascend.
With hearts and minds and voices we proclaim,
in summer days, the glory of your name.

Tom Gordon

Tiptoe through the tulips*

Tiptoe through the tulips,
peering at the pieris,
daft about the daffodils,
prancing in the primulas,
euphoric about the euphorbias,
dancing around the dandelions,
walking through the wallflowers,
butterflies on the buttercups
swell with the Sweet Williams,
ladybirds on the laburnum,
anguish over the antirrhinum,
God is in the godetia.
Dazing at the daisies,
marinating in the sun, the marigolds.
Narcotic, yes a bit, with the narcissus,
plentiful and pretty the pansies and petunias.
Hydrant, we need water for the hydrangea,
roses, posing in blossom, lovely roses.
Weeding, with a shovel, around the weeping willow,
scent coming from the scabious.

God is in our gardening.
God is in the garden.

Karen Kinloch

* Title of a song published in 1929, written by Al Dubin (lyrics) and Joe Burke (music).

For the sun's rising

For the sun's rising
and its beams of precious warmth,
Thanks be to you, O God.

For the morning's gleaming promise ... plants awakening,
flowers blooming, trees dancing in soft wind,
Thanks be to you, O God.

For the air, warm and wet with summer's invitation to
play and rest,
Thanks be to you, O God.

For the birds singing their returning song
and the fragile nests that hold new life,
Thanks be to you, O God.

For the noontime heat
and the refreshing lap of water on the shore,
Thanks be to you, O God.

For shoeless feet and toes
that wriggle in sand and grass,
Thanks be to you, O God.

For the long evenings
stretching out like a blanket of restful sleep,
Thanks be to you, O God.

For the brilliant blue-black of night sky,
silent stars dancing in flickering magic,
Thanks be to you, O God.

For the arc of this summer's day, and for all days,
our hearts are full to overflowing
with gratitude to you, Creator God.

Sally Howell Johnson

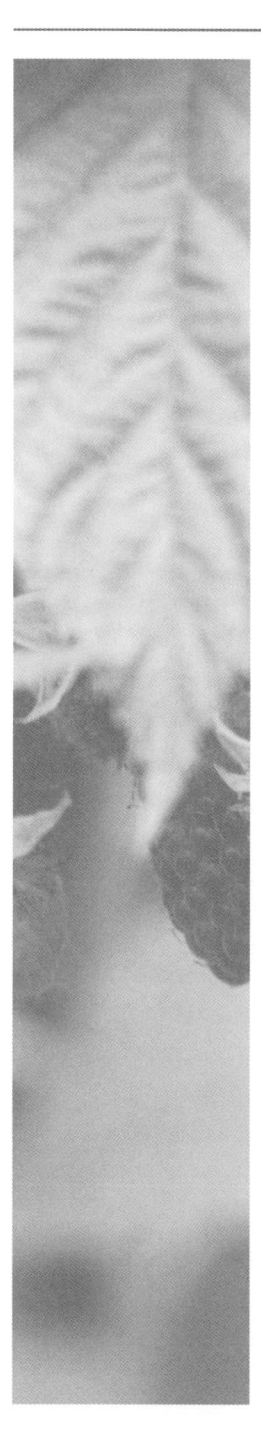

A summer visit to Flanders

No poppies here.
No summer flowers to stir the soul.
No thousands of visitors to pay their respects.
Just a couple of old friends
walking and looking at the grey tombs
of 'the enemy'.

No bright sunlight here
breaking through overhanging trees.
No white crosses,
no commemorations
for these 'other' fallen comrades.
It's as though
summer isn't welcome in this corner.

No open spaces here.
Just enclosed walls and fence.
Do the seasons discriminate?
Is this field fit only for the short days
and darkening skies?
Yet these men knew summer too
and love and passion
and happiness.
and fear.

When we deny even the sun to shine
on these long-lost graves
do we crucify Christ
again
and again
and again?

Alma Fritchley

Rainbow God

(A prayer for Pride)

Rainbow God,
we praise you that you have created us
as your embodied daughters and sons,
gay, straight, trans or bi.
We give you thanks for pleasure and desire,
for holy loving and tender care.
Rainbow God,
give us courage and pride
to celebrate today.

Rainbow God,
we praise you for our city,
welcoming diverse communities
of races, nations, abilities and sexualities.
We give you thanks for multicultural living,
transcending barriers and embracing diversity.
Rainbow God,
give us courage and pride
to affirm one another.

Rainbow God,
we grieve for the hurt and rejection
which have wounded so many of us
in family, community or church.
We ask for strength in facing the silencing and abuse
which deny our dignity and humanity.
Rainbow God,
give us courage and pride
to resist prejudice today.

Rainbow God,
we praise you for the richness of our faith,
affirming difference and diversity,
and acknowledging that of you in every living being.
We give you thanks for the glory of humanity
and the sense of worth of every individual.
**Rainbow God,
give us courage and pride
to celebrate today.**

Jan Berry

For sunlight dancing

For sunlight dancing on white-crested waves,
Creative God, we offer our thanks and praise.

For sunlight dappling forest glades,
Creative God, we offer our thanks and praise.

For sunlight gilding wheat and maize,
Creative God, we offer our thanks and praise.

For sunlight lengthening summer days,
Creative God, we offer our thanks and praise.

Avis Palmer

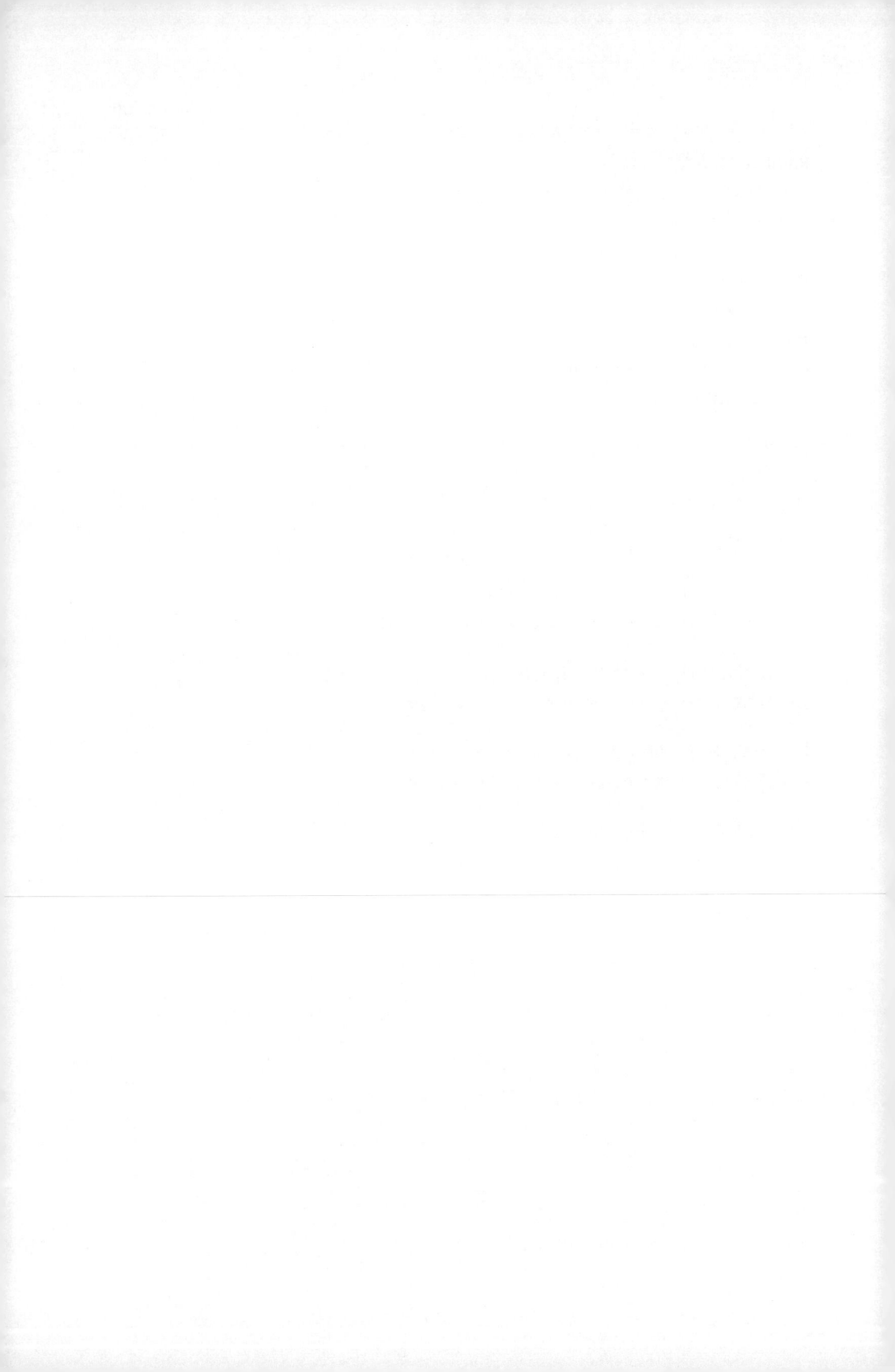

Summer saints

As children to a mother

(A prayer for Julian's Day, 13th May)

God of love, we come to you
as children to a mother,
confident and sure in your love,
trusting in your welcome and protection.

God of compassion, we come to you
as children to a mother,
running from our hurt and fear
into the safety of your arms.

God of hope, we come to you
as children to a mother,
knowing we will live and grow
in oneness with you.

God of all life,
you have made us as your children;
gather us into your arms in love,
keep us from harm,
hold us in love;
and may we know that in you
'all shall be well,
and all manner of things shall be well'.

Jan Berry

Remembering Julian

(Tune: 'Nun danket'/'Now thank we all our God')

'Come now and follow me';
to us Christ's words are spoken.
He calls each one by name;
by Love our hearts are woken.
We're asked to walk with faith

a path we cannot tell;
and well shall all things be,
and all things shall be well.

We learn a different way
through Christ in us abiding.
Forgiveness sets us free
to trust in Love's providing.
Christ's empathy and peace
our doubts and fears dispel;
and well shall all things be,
and all things shall be well.

Our journey is our song
of words and deeds and silence.
We know Christ through our friends:
his care, his joy, his guidance.
We seek, and find by grace,
it is in Love we dwell;
and well shall all things be,
and all things shall be well.

Avis Palmer

Eucharistic prayer of thanksgiving for Julian's Day

God, the wellspring of our days,
we praise you for the world you have made,
with all its delight and beauty,
its tenderness and joy.

God, the source of wisdom,
we praise you for your love for us,
embracing us like a father,
reaching out to us like a mother,
enfolding us in compassion.

God, the breath of all that is,
we praise you for the way you keep us,
holding us through pain and hurt,
enclosing us in kindness.
And so we join in the song of all creation,
praising you and saying,
Holy, Holy, Holy God,
who makes all things well
and in whom all shall be well;
blessed be your name.

As we take this bread and wine,
may our trust be restored,
our courage strengthened
and our hope renewed
until we find ourselves
one with you and the whole created world.
Amen

Jan Berry

All will be well

(A Mother Julian reflection)

*'All will be well
and all manner of things
will be well.'*

All, everything, the sun and moon,
pyjamas and bed jacket,
bedtime story and candlelight,
game of chase, scary novel,
black-and-white certainties,
mystery and misty fields.

All manner of things, you say:
dark alleyway,
unmapped forest,
relentless storm,
blue-tinged frost.

All manner of things, you say:
the hectic meeting,
raised voices,
bustle and vision,
clamour of diary,
argument and puzzle,
the lonely voice,
the broken and lost

All manner of things, you say;
all manner of things will be well,
will be heard, held, accepted,
given the gift of space,
given the answer of love,
given the space to dream,
shown a way forward,
lit by God's flame,
stilled like the calming of the waves.

*'All will be well
and all manner of things
will be well.'*

Judy Dinnen

The monk from Jarrow

As the local metro train paused at the station,
young children, reading the sign,
shouted: 'Bede! Bede!'
The words struck my soul.

Close by
nestled near the sleepy river Don
lies the land of Bede.
A sacred space.
Timeless.
Generations of my family alone
have followed in Bede's footsteps.

Bede the monk from Jarrow:
historian,
poet,
scientist,
musician,
theologian,
man of the stars.

Bede the monk from Jarrow,
given by the church
the title Venerable.

Long may children shout his name
and come to learn of his loves and life.

Sarah Pascoe

Aldersgate Sunday

Celebrated nearest to 24th May, the anniversary of John Wesley's 'warmed heart'.

O God, who raised up the people called Methodists
to spread scriptural holiness throughout the land,
renew us with your Spirit of grace and justice,
that hearts may be warmed
and the world changed
to reflect that New Jerusalem
towards which we travel in hope and longing.
Through Jesus our brother, our companion and our Lord. Amen

Richard Sharples

A heart strangely warmed

(Aldersgate Sunday, 24th May)

The day the founder of Methodism, John Wesley, had a personal experience of God's love.

In an unexpected time
in an ordinary place
God's Word
became flesh
and took flight
in a heart strangely warmed.

Dynamic Spirit of God,
when our faith burns low
when our prayers are scarce
when our worship is dull routine
wake us up!

Open our minds and hearts
to discover you anew,
warming hearts,
transforming lives,
assuring us of your love.

Fill us with the vitality of your Spirit,
fire us with your passion and life,
enliven us to your living presence:
make every moment
a dance with you. Amen

Louise Gough

Heroes

A stone was where Cuchulain laid his head,
round which, as sagas tell, played hero-light;
a thousand could not best him in the fight,
and ev'n his horse shed tears when he was dead.

So too Columba: match for pagan might;
a stone as pillow for his hero's rest;
horse weeping its farewell against his breast;
head haloed in unearthly radiance bright.

Praise to both heroes. One, doomed to descend
from sun-god origins to mortal end,
shouts, by his deeds, that death must be defied;

the other, although sprung from mortal line,
is upwards drawn to mirror the divine:
mortal life's end – becoming deified.

James Munro

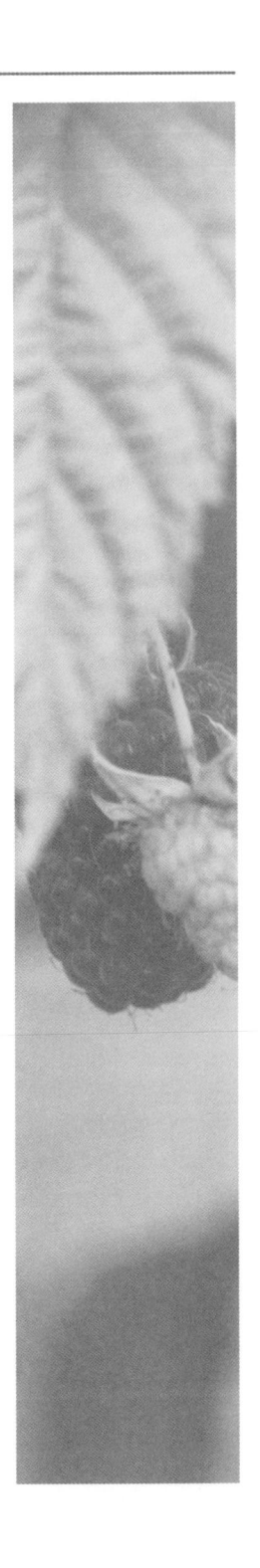

Prayer for St Columba's Day

Lord, grant the least of all your servants,
bound soon to leave this troubled shore;
I claim no right to see your glory,
but let me keep your furthest door.

The roughest wood, the darkest gateway;
the meanest door, the least gone through;
the utmost edge of Heaven's dominion:
and know that there, I still serve you.

See: https://soundcloud.com/roddy-6/columbas-prayer

Roddy Cowie

Saint Pat and Saint Colum

(Tune: 'The soldier's prayer', English traditional)

Saint Pat and Saint Colum were walking one day.
Says Patrick to Colum, 'Come, let us pray.
And if we have one prayer, may we also have ten.'
'Let's have the full breastplate,' says Columba. 'Amen.'

'What shall we pray for?' 'Let's pray for the poor.
Two thousand million at the rich man's front door.'
'If we change that in one way, let's change it in ten.'
'Let's have a revolution,' says Columba. 'Amen.'

'What shall we pray for?' 'We'll pray for the Church.'
'Why should we?' said Pat. 'They left us in the lurch.
If the wild Spirit moved them, they'd move back again.'
'They're a wet bunch of heathens,' says Columba. 'Amen.'

'What shall we pray for?' 'Let's pray for the earth.'
'You're right there,' says Patrick, 'for all that we're worth.
If it's mangled in one way, it's mangled in ten.'
'Who'd think that God made it?' says Columba. 'Amen.'

'What shall we pray for?' 'Let's pray for our own,
who stand up and speak before armies and thrones.'
'The stubbornest women and awkwardest men.'
'Aye, much like ourselves,' says Columba. 'Amen.'

Roddy Cowie

It's hard to enter the kingdom

(A song for St Peter, Mark 10:23–30)

(Tune: 'The four Marys')

'It's hard to enter the Kingdom,
and if you're rich and great
it's like a heavy-loaded beast
stuck in a narrow gate.'

Then Peter says to Jesus,
'You frighten me to death –
I've left my home and everything,
and I have nothing left.'

'It's hard to enter the Kingdom,
you know that I have tried,
but at the end, when you go through,
will I be left outside?'

'Oh, Peter, Peter,' Jesus said,
'what will I do with you?
I tell you: God will get you there
if he has to drag you through.'

Roddy Cowie

See: https://soundcloud.com/roddy-6/the-camel-through-the-needle

St Swithun was here

Antiphons and anthems,
banners all down the nave,
petitions and processions,
priests pacing over graves,
the organ with all stops out
and sonorous Latin prayers,
but for all that pomp and circumstance
St Swithun isn't there.

No body in a sepulchre,
no relic on display,
no sign, no shrine:
scepticism and time
have swept the trace away.
Once folk felt his presence
in this city – come rain, come shine –
but history's stolen the evidence,
and under exultant arches
the paving stones lie bare –
St Swithun's now not there.

Only a crowd of worshippers
offering an obscure prayer;
hopeful holy people
blessing the empty air.

Jan Sutch Pickard

This was written in Winchester Cathedral, where a shrine was built over the relics of St Swithun, an Anglo Saxon Bishop, patron saint of the city, who was buried there. Since the Reformation, there has been no trace of his shrine, though legends of healing survive. There's also a tradition of weather forecasting connected to his Feast Day, 15 July, when there's a special service.

Holy Fools

(For 1st July, the Feast of St Simeon, the Holy Fool)

Today is All Fools' Day.
People come into church
dancing in their suits,
red, blue and green in their prayers,
speaking in the tongues of
donkeys, cows and horses,
singing in the voice of a bassoon,
praying like a bagpipe.
People dance with ribbons
and tie prayers into knots
of many colours.

Flowers grow in the font.
A river snakes down the aisle.
Incense chuckles.
Bells hiccup.
Books dance
and the words fall out
laughing.

Today is All Fools' Day.
A woman speaks with her hands;
she is a holy clown,
rainbow thief,
bird woman.
She meets a snake man
who prays with stories.

Today is All Fools' Day.
People fly out of church
spilling words,
untangling songs,
fools, clowns and rainbow thieves.

Judy Dinnen

Summer holidays

A teacher's prayers at the end of a school year

During exams and tests:

Jesus, who was tested,
help me to see the precious spark of God's wonderful creation
in each of these children.
Help me to show them that their infinite value
is so much more than a mark in a test.
Help me, when I too am judged by test scores,
to know my value is so much more than this too. Amen

Saying goodbye to a class:

Jesus, who grew in wisdom and stature,
be with these children
as they take the next step in life's journey.
On this, our last day together,
I name in my heart those for whom this step will be difficult.
I rage at a society that fails the children I have cared for,
remembering especially those living in poverty
who will miss their free school meal.

(Take a few moments to bring before God those for whom this time will be hard.)

I lament the loss of 'my kids'.
They are moving on and will not need me now in the same way.
It's hard to let go.
I remember and rejoice in the great times we have had together,
and confess the times of struggle and weakness.

(Take a few moments to remember this school year before God.)

My work here is now complete.
Bless these children,
and those now charged with their care.
Amen

A prayer for clearing out a classroom:

Jesus, whose kingdom is like a woman who swept a room to find a coin,
as I clear the clutter, and carefully store away the things I will need again,
help me not to be overwhelmed by stuff.
Help me, too, to clear away the clutter in my life,
and to treasure all that is valuable.

I put away stress.
I put away blame and negativity.
I treasure the lessons I have learned and the sparks of inspiration.

As I close the door and leave this school year behind,
I take one last look and dedicate this classroom
to continue to be a place of love, care and the joy of learning new things.
Amen

A prayer about summer holidays:

Jesus, the teacher who took himself off to a quiet place away from the crowds,
I embrace the opportunity now to renew myself.
May I draw deeply from the well of creation's abundance,
be nourished in mind, body and spirit,
and return to begin my ministry anew,
refreshed and re-created.
Amen

Liz Delafield

God of holidays

For rest and relaxation,
switching off phones and e-mail,
the release from the demands of diaries and calendars,
the blissful luxury of solitude.
God who rests with us,
for holiday joys, we praise you.

For travel and exploration,
adventuring to new places,
discovering beauty and strangeness,
exploring new food and ways of life.
God who travels with us,
for holiday joys, we praise you.

For play and leisure,
games on beach or field,
delighting in fun and laughter,
sharing time with friends.
God who plays with us,
for holiday joys, we praise you.

For making and creating,
forming shapes in clay, wood or stone,
splashing colour with paint or thread,
words or music echoing in our souls.
God who creates with us,
for holiday joys, we praise you.

Jan Berry

A very British summer

Excitement as someone is the first to see the sea
and dad grumpy cos there's nowhere near it
to park the overloaded car.

Feeling the softness of sand
under our feet and between our toes,
and its crunch in our sandwiches munched on the beach.

Sheltering from sudden summer rain
under the shade that we thought we'd bought
to protect us from the sun.

Enjoying an outdoor lunch,
but keeping a watchful eye
on the gull that wants to nick your chips.

Savouring an ice cream out on the seafront
with mint choc chip, raspberry ripple
and a pesky wasp that wants to share the treat.

So here we are out together in God's good earth,
experiencing a very British summer.
It's character-building and memory-making,
the source of many a story on a winter's night

Simon Taylor

We thank you

Creator God,
we praise you for the birth of summer,
warmth and light,
brightness and colour.
May we rejoice in your rainbow world.

Redeeming Son,
we thank you for sunshine and showers,
rest and relaxation,
recreation and holidays.
May we be refreshed with energy and hope.

Guiding Spirit,
we bless you for family and friends,
fellowship and company,
freedom to worship and pray.
May we be renewed with your love and grace.

Ruth Bowen

Two whole months of glorious freedom

Thanks be to God
for the last meeting of the church year,
the final 'Amen' of the final benediction
signalling the start of two whole months
of glorious freedom …
… freedom from:
mission strategies and vision statements;
counter-motions, points of order and addenda;
hidden agendas and open hostilities;
leaky roofs and squeaky organs and
'Who moved the Guild teapot?';

hobby horses and elephants in the room;
too much talking and not enough listening;
and an intense interest in the pattern on the carpet
when volunteers are needed;
watching the hands on the clock move round, ever so slowly;
wondering what Jesus would make of it all.

J Mary Henderson

Down at the harbour

Down at Portsoy*
the Festival in full swing:
large historic boats,
traditional sailing boats,
wee modern boats,
cheer on local skiffs,
Viking torch-lit parades.

Food and drink aplenty,
music and crafts at the Green,
all fun and laughter.

I believe God is not anti-fun
for we are his finite creatures,
and God created us to rest, recharge and rejuvenate –
God created us to enjoy life.

Mary Whittaker

* There's a traditional boat festival at Portsoy, a town in Aberdeenshire, every June.

Journeys

Toddling forward

Toddling forward,
running down the path.
A breeze blowing tulips and the last of the daffodils.
'Look, Adam! The flowers are dancing.'
He stops and scans the whole garden,
begins to move his arms and legs,
wiggles his torso.
Smiling up at me,
dancing with the flowers.

Mary Hanrahan

Journey on the roads in Cameroon

In the car

A black chicken in a bag,
a box of cheeping chicks,
a red cabbage,
two red-and-yellow tunics from Bamendi,
four musical shakers,
a loaf of bread.

Things carried on heads

A suitcase with wheels,
a comfy armchair,
a tree trunk,
a tray of bananas,
a white sack of carrots,
a basket of washing,
a red casserole dish,
a flask of palm oil,
a box with eggs in,
twenty coloured buckets.

*Dead things on a stick**

A snake,
a cane rat,
a polecat,
a stripy cat.

Seen on the road

A mattress on the back of a bike,
a cart of tomatoes and beans,
a truck piled high and four people
sitting on top of the vegetable sacks,
dos d'ânes ('sleeping policemen').

Seen by the roadside

An upside-down lorry,
buckets of cabbages,
men washing motorbikes in a stream,
a little girl in a red hat and fur coat,
a café called Noces de Cana,
a brown-and-white goat,
a woman taking cassava from a sack,
a soldier in a red cap dusting his car,
a stall of clothes irons and one of mirrors,
two men carrying a pane of glass,
a lorry saying *'Tout à Dieu'*,
a termite mound,
a bush covered with drying clothes,
a boy with a sewing machine on his shoulder,
two pink-and-black piglets,
a pink church with a spire.

Judy Dinnen

* *Sold at the edge of the road as meat*

The red scooter

The shiny red mobility scooter was the first thing to grab our attention – the second was the generous smile of the driver, as he glided slowly into the queue for the restaurant.

Judith exclaimed, 'Now that's a well-polished glistening red scooter – I've never seen one so beautiful.'

'Don't you love it?!' said the man, whose name was Don. 'I can't walk any more, I can't drive any more, but I finally have my childhood dream. I'm in my 80s – and I finally have a red scooter.' He glowed with gusto, glistened with gratitude.

Suzi, Don's wife, came into the line, and then we were pleasingly seated together, two couples who had never met but shared life stories and struggles.

At one point in the conversation I turned to Don and said, 'I want you to know that from the first moment we met this evening, I was grateful and pleased. I think you are a new mentor for me. I believe the biggest spiritual challenge for those of us who are ageing is how we cope with losses – they keep coming faster and hitting more deeply. If it is not some part of our body failing, it is that someone dear to us is lost by death or distance. We begin to lose the activities that gave our lives richness. All the losses we encounter are a challenge. From the instant you came up to us, you communicated your losses and your continued vitality, guts, resilience, hope, good humour and lust for life. You witness gratitude and joy! For that I am very grateful.'

Don appeared a little stunned; then he smiled and said a quiet, 'Thank you.'

I have a new friend – a new mentor. He drives a red scooter!

Benjamin Pratt

Mom's feet

*How beautiful on the mountains
    are the feet of those who bring good news,
who proclaim peace,
    who bring good tidings ... (Isaiah 52:7, NIV)*

Mom's feet
have travelled up the side of Mt Kilimanjaro
walked on the sands of the Indian Ocean
navigated airports on most every continent
huffed along cobblestone streets in Portugal
felt the summer sun of Diamond Lake
and the icy-cold snow of many Minnesota winters.

Mom's feet
have sprinted after grandchildren
tiptoed beside the bed as her beloved momma met Jesus
entered countless chapels and synagogues and prayer rooms
to worship her Beloved
have sweated in mud huts
laboured along dusty trails
treaded rocky paths
stood for hours at a time
to bring life and hope and promise.

Mom's feet
tell story after story after story
kicking balls
playing hopscotch
walking down a road to visit a friend
loving life
loving others
loving Jesus.

Mom's feet
beautiful and brittle with years and arthritis
beautiful and entombed with neuropathy

with pain in every step
tell story after story after story
sorrow and joy
pain and love
death and life.

Mom's beautiful
beautiful feet.

I want feet just like my mom's.

Becky Grisell

It's a funny old journey

It's a funny old journey,
the journey of faith.
Does faith change or do we?
Those things that seemed so important
when we started out
have given way to other issues.
The deal-breakers
become the room-makers,
the passions we held
become mellowed
by the passage of time
as we learn and grow,
as our hearts swell with love.

And as we begin to understand better
the God who lives beside us,
the God who will not be fettered
by any limits
that we place
on compassion.
The God who calls us
to ignore the limits too.

The God who promises that, one day,
it will all become clear.

But, until then,
we should carry on loving
along the way.
It's a funny old journey.

Liz Crumlish, Spill the Beans

Travel with me

Travel with me, God.
Sit down beside me
and watch the world through
the train window.

Speak to me
through the people I meet.

Walk with me
into tower blocks
and forests.

Listen to me
when I'm happy
and when I'm sad.

Travel with me, God,
going out,
coming in,
heading homewards.

Travel with me
to and beyond the end,
whatever the end may be.

Ruth Burgess

I am still with you

'I come to the end – I am still with you.' Psalm 139:18b (NRSV)

No shadowed alley
but well-lighted streets,

no angry words,
but whispers of love,

no wretched punishment,
but warm embraces,

no anguished emptiness,
but a heart filled with hope,

just beyond the end.

Thom M Shuman

Pilgrimage and retreat

I search for you

I search for you in the bleak beauty of Kinder
and you hide from me.
I wild camp in cold and rain,
but still you do not come.

I walk in busy Dovedale,
climb up Thorpe Cloud to get away from the crowd,
but still you stay away.

I look down on the River Dove,
and ponder jumping.
I hallucinate instead the smell of sausages and beans
heating on my primus stove.
I've not eaten for days.
I rush to camp to satisfy that hunger.

With exhaustion and food within me I sleep,
the first good sleep for weeks.
Rested, I plan my last day's trek:
work calls tomorrow.

I rage for a moment – God still has not come
and I'll go back with the conflict
and anxiety dictating everything I came to change.
Then I think of all the lonely, lost and hungry people in the world.
I am so lucky. I have freedom to roam.
Some flee brutal regimes to try to get to ours.
I pray to God to help them.
He has real need to be with them.

Maybe I expect too much from God?
I need to sort my conflict.
I've got a job, friends and family.

I walk with a spring in my step.

Then I come to the River Manifold.
I need its bearing to navigate.
It's not there, just a dry riverbed.

I rage, swear and cry from the pit of my soul:
'God! Why are you hiding?!
Why are you laughing at me?
Why do you play games?'
I realise I have shouted out loud.
I look round but there is only me.

Then God is there, unexpectedly,
telling me he loves me and why didn't I call him before?
And I laugh and cry in peace, joy and forgiveness.
I am part of his creation.
It is as if I've just been born.

He's come to my trivial need.
I can't thank and praise him enough.
He laughs too.

Robert Shooter

The cove

(Remembering a Devon childhood)

There was only one track to its waters.
Always steep.
Always slow.
Each step a hesitation.
Then
a wonder would lie before us,
always sunlit
always still
as the cove waited to receive us.

It was the place
where I first
jumped in from the rocks,
swam out of my depth
and stroked her hair.
A thrilling place.
Always sunlit,
always still
as the cove embraced us.

A place of learning, of growing, of changing;
but above all
a place of gathering.
A gathering place for the people
who tread the track
to arrive
always at the same place,
always at the same time.
Rocks would serve as pews
and the cove became a chapel.

And songs would be the lapping of waves on the rising tide,
and prayer the whisper of a breeze
and the sermon would be a silence,
resting in stories remembered without the retelling.

John Rackley

St Queran's Well, Troqueer

This is a green place,
trees, thistles, nettles,
a place of power,
a place to go barefoot,
a place of prayer.

Here yellow leaves float and dance,
bubbles surface and burst.

This water is cold.
Clean cold,
stone cold,
pure cold and holy.
The earth's warmth shivers here.

This is a place of meeting,
a whole place,
a place of healing.

Celt of water,
Christ of earth,
touch me,
wash me clean.

Keep me in holiness
through my nights
and days.

Ruth Burgess

Malta retreat

Malta retreat – beginning

The noise of traffic
searing, relentless, urgent, demanding attention,
the world is here too.

I am in the world
of noise, of traffic, of roaring planes.

Yet over the threshold still
the birds sing high in the trees,
the fragrance of perfume lingers
and welcomes me in.

Welcomes us in, to I know not what
except I know it is good to be here,
to rest in Oneness,
for a while to linger,
to be resourced,
to be made ready,

to carry the beauty and joy of our Compassionate God
across the threshold
into the world
when called.

Malta retreat – ending

Here we are, coming to the end of our retreat.
The noise of traffic and planes has receded.
The birds still sing.
Here we are, within the vast blue sky, pulsating universe.
Here beside the ripening barley, gently swaying in the breeze,
rippling, ready, reaching to give its all.

Here we are.
Here we have come.
From here we will go.

New light is streaming up over the horizon.
The blue sky tells of the vastness of God – infinite, deep, spacious,
holding all my unanswered questions.
I am held in this vastness.

We are held, connected, joining hands,
each a tiny, unique, precious, infinitely loved part of creation.
I am, we are, 'from love, of love, for love'.
Our brokenness, our wounded hands held
in the risen Christ's wounded, strong, healing hands.

So take our hands
to bless
and to be a blessing …

The blessing of the love of the Creator be ours,
the blessing of the wounded and risen Christ be ours,
the blessing of the Spirit of new life be ours.

Be ours
and be with all those we love,
and all those we pray for.

Helen Kinloch

The well

Silently I prepare.
Walking along an old path beside a murmuring brook,
barefoot, touching our Mother, the earth.
Every step a sacred step: love, peace, joy, happiness.
A pool in the small brook appears.

I undress and emerge myself in the cold water,
closing my nose I go under, 3 times down, 3 times up,
and leave the pool on the other side.
On a stone a simple cotton dress awaits.
I dress myself,
and continue.

Under the old oak
the water bubbles up gently.
Clear transparent water.
I bow in reverence.
Tears run down my face.
Slowly I drink from the wooden bowl left there,
quenching a thirst unknown.

I place flowers and stones found along the path.
A song comes from my lips,
a song from my soul,
and joins the rustling leaves.
Branches sway softly.

Peace-full I continue the journey.

Roberta van Biezen

Chester Cathedral*

Here is no slender eloquence reaching up to pierce the heavens.
No stone filigree beams the light of heaven through
soaring flying buttresses.
Here is a solid, dependable place
alive with the ever-moving changelessness of God.

Here is a place where saturated stones drip with prayer
and the silent music of praise rings around the roof bosses.
Here is a place where the stamp and tramp of pilgrims' feet
echo round the pillars and down the cloisters of the years.

Here the elements of bread and wine feed the soul of shifting humanity
and tea and cake sustain the body;
the both made whole within these living stones.

Here the world's conductors nourish the spirits of a multitude of ears.

Here the firm authority of Episcopal hands
confirm the faithful with the Holy Spirit
and ordain the chosen to Apostolic succession.

And so it is, amongst these living, breathing stones,
that the world works and prays and worships and plays.
Gathered into the timeless changelessness of God,
secure and safe in this solid, living frame.

S Anne Lawson

This is a very personal view of Chester Cathedral. For over 30 years, the cathedral has been for me a place of worship, rest and refreshment; it has also been a concert hall, as I've been privileged to perform in concerts and recordings in the cathedral. Perhaps most importantly, it is the place where I was ordained.

Back where I started

Cold coiling tentacles curling around
mind, heart and throat, pulled down nearly drowned,
I break from ice fingers, slip from the snare,
kick to the surface gasping for air.

Startled and stumbled, looking for light,
chose the wrong road because of poor sight,
drenched by betrayal, punched in the gut,
crawled to the door, the door was slammed shut.

Detaching from drama and my epitaph,
kindling light, and sometimes a laugh,
learned to not care, that I may care more,
to leave from small rooms, through a locked door.

Now nothing to do, nothing to lose,
walked all the paths, wore out my shoes,
travelled strange lands, on rough roads uncharted,
now with no plans I'm back where I started.

Back where I started, no braces, no belts,
back where I started, there is nowhere else.
Back in the silence that fits like a glove,
believing in nothing, knowing God's love.

Stuart Barrie

There is a Christ, and he sails the storm

(Tune: 'Waly, waly')

There is a Christ, and he sails the storm,
as he has sailed two thousand years;
we see him dimly through the rain,
confused with our own doubts and fears.

Where one will see a working man,
another hears a mystic's voice,
and one will see a wedding guest,
and one a suffering sacrifice.

For some you are the living sea,
for some you seem a burning star.
Teach us to trust each other's sight,
until we see you as you are.

Roddy Cowie

Summer blessings

An all-day summer blessing

May birds fill the dawn of your day with song,
may the midday sun caress your face with warmth,
may honeysuckle scent the evening breeze around you
and may the summer stars shine bright above you.

And may God,
the giver of summer song and scent,
the Creator of the sun and stars,
touch your life with beauty
and fill your heart with joy.
Amen

Simon Taylor

Bless all who worship you

(Tune: 'Geistliche Kirchengesänge'/'All creatures of our God and King', arranged by Ralph Vaughan Williams)

Bless all who worship you, O God,
from praise at dawn to sunset song;
from your goodness, you enrich us.
Oh, by your love, inspire us.
Oh, by your Spirit, guide us.
By your power, you protect us.
In your mercy, you receive us,
now and always

da Noust

May God our Creator

May God our Creator hold you and yours in the arms of his love.
May Jesus inspire you in your loving and serving.
May the Spirit guide you as you journey onwards.
In the name of the Trinity of grace.
Amen

Simon Taylor

The blessing of the God of life

The blessing of the quiet earth,
upholding you, strengthening you.

The blessing of the wind that blows,
inspiring you, exciting you.

The blessing of the fire that burns,
warming you, refining you.

The blessing of the water that flows,
delighting you, refreshing you.

The blessing of the God of life,
whom we come to know in Christ,
and who lives in us through the Spirit,
be yours this day, and always. Amen

Richard Sharples

A joyful summer blessing

May God bless you
with a warm day
and a comfy sun-lounger.

May God bless you
with a good book,
a cold drink
and a choc-ice.

May God bless you
with a work-free afternoon
and the joy of summer.

Ruth Burgess

God bless

God bless the bees:
the bees that pollinate my plum tree,
the bees that bump into my conservatory windows,
the bees that work in my friend's hives and produce sweet honey.

God bless the worms:
the worms that turn the soil over,
the worms that help weeds and vegetables grow,
the worms that sometimes provide the birds with dinner.

God bless the butterflies:
the butterflies that herald summer,
the butterflies that dance in the sunlight,
even the butterflies that lay eggs in my cabbages.

God bless the wee creatures
in our gardens.

Ruth Burgess

May long summer days

May long summer days
speak to you of God's enduring light.

May bright summer flowers
speak to you of God's unending beauty.

May fresh summer fruits
speak to you of God's continuing kindness.

May warm summer nights
speak to you of God's enfolding comfort.

May early summer dawns
speak to you of God's renewing hope.

Simon Taylor

Sources

'Flesh, blood, bones' is taken from *Recognition: Discover Yourself at the Heart of the Story*, by Janet Killeen, Amazon/Kindle, 2019. Used by permission of Janet Killeen

'What did you expect?', by Kit Walkman, was first published on Worship Cloud. Used by permission of Kit Walkman

'An elemental Rogation liturgy', by Ruth Burgess, was revised from the version in *Cherish the Earth: Reflections on a Living Planet*, Mary Low, Wild Goose Publications, 2004

'Highland morning' was first published in *Reflections of Life: Words of Comfort and Encouragement*, published by NHS Education for Scotland. Used by permission of Peter Millar

'In the world, God's love declaring', by Jan Berry, was first published in *Naming God*, by Jan Berry, Granary, a URC Publication, 2011. Used by permission of Jan Berry

Spill the Beans material © the contributors. Spill the Beans is 'a lectionary-based resource with a Scottish flavour for Sunday Schools, Junior Churches and worship leaders': http://spillbeans.org.uk

Scripture quotations taken from The Holy Bible, New International Version® NIV® Copyright © 1973 1978 1984 2011 by Biblica, Inc. TM Used by permission. All rights reserved worldwide.

Scripture quotation from the New Revised Standard Version Bible, copyright © 1989 the Division of Christian Education of the National Council of the Churches of Christ in the United States of America. Used by permission. All rights reserved.

About the authors

Angie Allport is a Deacon in the Methodist Church and a member of the Methodist Diaconal Order, which has a Rule of life. Angie served in Harpenden before recently moving to a new appointment in Hereford.

Gill Bailey: 'I am a Nationally Accredited Lay Preacher working in the Wessex Synod. I have recently gained an MA in 'Theology, Imagination and Culture' at Sarum College, which I hope will help me to be more informed, relevant and imaginative in my ministry.'

Helen Barrett: 'I am a Methodist Local Preacher and my other main interests are justice and peace issues, particularly the natural world and fairtrade.'

Stuart Barrie: 'Born in Govan, Glasgow, then moved to East Kilbride where I spent my working life as an aero engineer in Rolls-Royce. An engineer by necessity, a poet by inclination, with a soft heart (well-defended).'

Elizabeth Baxter continues into her 28th year as part of the vibrant, therapeutic and theological community of Holy Rood House in Thirsk. Through her ministry as priest, theologian and liturgist she enjoys accompanying people on their therapeutic and spiritual journeys, and exploring the shift-shaping of an ecological vision offering hope for the future for individuals, communities and the earth.

Jan Berry lives in Northwich, Cheshire, with her partner, where she enjoys walking by the river, creative writing and circle dancing. She is a 'retired' minister of the United Reformed Church, but keeps herself occupied by offering spiritual accompaniment, retreats and quiet days and workshops.

Keith Blackwood is Minister at Mannofield Church, Aberdeen.

Ruth Bowen is a retired special needs teacher. She lived and worked in Stronsay, Orkney, but now lives nearer her son in Clevedon with her husband, David. She enjoys gardening, wool crafts and spending time with family and friends.

Ruth Burgess is a member of the Iona Community living in Dunblane. She enjoys being retired, growing fruit, flowers and vegetables, writing and paddling along the seashore whenever possible.

Rev. Scott Burton is parish minister in West Kintyre and the Isle of Gigha Church of Scotland. He has written a book called *Holy Whitewater* – on the spirituality of kayaking, and enjoys writing prayers and reflections for worship.

Elizabeth Clark is a Methodist minister and is currently the National Rural Officer for the Methodist and United Reformed Churches. She loves the countryside and is passionate about rural churches and their ministry.

Roddy Cowie is a retired professor of psychology and a lay reader in the Church of Ireland. He is an associate of the Community, and yearly time on Iona has always been part of his life, with parents, then children, then grandchildren.

Kathy Crawford is a Reader in the Diocese of Southwell and Nottingham. In her spare time she enjoys creative writing, gardening, baking and doing word puzzles.

Liz Crumlish is a writer and poet, passionate about amplifying the voices of women and making room for all at God's table. She blogs at www.liz-vicarof-dibley.blogspot.com

da Noust are an informal ensemble of members and friends of L'Arche Edinburgh, a community of people with and without learning disabilities. Musical settings of their texts are on their YouTube channel: da Noust.

Liz Delafield is a Primary school teacher, living in Stockport, Greater Manchester with her family Stewart, Jennifer and Robert. She is an associate member of the Iona Community.

Judy Dinnen lives in beautiful Herefordshire, where she writes and ministers in local churches. After many years as an associate, she is delighted to belong to an Iona Cymru Family Group in Abergavenny.

Carol Dixon was born in Alnwick, Northumberland and is a lay preacher in the United Reformed Church and a Friend of St Cuthbert's, Lindisfarne, for whom she produced a CD of Holy Island hymns. Her prayers and hymns are in HymnQuest, the URC Prayer Handbook and the Church of Scotland hymnbook (CH4) and she also writes for the international Christian blog godspacelight.com. She is a wife, mother and grandmother and enjoys touring with her husband in their caravette.

Paul Fillery: Paul worked as an osteopath for 32 years and was ordained as a priest in the Church of England in 2011. He now serves as a parish priest in Sandford, near Crediton, Devon, where he lives with his wife Tracey and their dog Finn.

Brian Ford: 'I am a retired biology teacher, at present studying for an MA in theology. Apart from church activities, my hobbies are gardening, folk music and amateur theatre.'

About the authors

Alma Fritchley is an MA student at Luther King House theology college in Manchester. Last year she was ordained into NSM Ministry with the United Reformed Church and continues to work as Chaplain for Methodist Homes. She is married to Jan and they recently moved to Northwich, Cheshire.

Terry Garley studied English, French, German and Latin, before becoming a language teacher, and later a County Ecumenical Officer. Terry says: 'Language has always been a fascination. Finding expression for our views, understandings or opinions meets so many human needs. Hopefully it conveys not only our personal values but also appreciation of other perspectives.'

Tom Gordon is retired from hospice chaplaincy and parish ministry. He now writes hymns and reflective material, and facilitates bereavement support programmes in Edinburgh and East Lothian.

Louise Gough is a Methodist Presbyter currently serving the Manchester and Stockport District. She enjoys playing her flute and dancing, being by the sea, and time spent with her large cat Wesley.

Liz Gregory-Smith lives with her husband in New Brancepeth, a village on the edge of Durham City. She is a retired teacher and a Reader in the local Anglican Church. She has three delightful small grandchildren to whom visits are a priority in her life.

Dr Becky Grisell is a Spiritual Director and Supervisor, writer and founder and curator of Cascade Ministries (www.cascadeministries.org). Her approach to Spiritual Direction is holistic, addressing the brokenness of life while focusing on the hope of the Gospel. You can contact her directly at becky@cascadeministries.org

Roddy Hamilton likes a good story and in retelling it finding that moment when you come across an idea you didn't know was there before but must have been lurking, waiting …

Mary Hanrahan: 'I am an active parishioner of St Paul the Apostle RC Church in Shettleston, Glasgow. I enjoy reading, writing, card-making and a questioning faith.'

Pam Hathorn: 'I am someone waiting for the kingdom and trying to be wise, patient and prayerful so as not to miss the daily signs of its presence. I like to drink coffee in my garden too.'

J Mary Henderson: Recently retired Church of Scotland minister. Looking forward to living by the seaside – and not attending church meetings.

Dr Brian Hick has been a music critic and writer for fifty years, alongside his work as a Special Educational Needs consultant. He has written poetry throughout this time and published widely, including the Lark series, and runs the music website Lark Reviews.

Jean Hudson: 'I am a retired Methodist minister, enjoying our new bungalow with husband John and our 16-year-old dog Amy and making new friends. Time is happily filled, in or out of lockdown, with writing, spinning, baking, growing herbs and salad and contributing to both gathered and scattered worship.'

Ian (aged 7): 'Ian was in a class I taught in Sunderland in the 1990s. I loved his poetry.' (Ruth Burgess)

Sally Howell Johnson is a retired United Methodist minister living in St Paul, MN, USA. She is the author of *Barefoot Zone* and *The Practicing Life: Simple Acts, Sacred Living* (Kirk House) and writes a blog called Pause at sallyhowelljohnson.com

Peter Johnston is minister of Ferryhill Parish Church of Scotland, editor of Spill the Beans resource books, and enjoys experimenting with worship. He is a musician and dog walker.

Janet Killeen, retired from teaching, is involved with the community of her church, St George's, in southeast London. She writes poetry and short stories, including the collection *Recognition* and a novel *After the Flood*, which will be followed this summer by its sequel, *Release the Raven*.

Helen Kinloch: Long retired from social work and related jobs. Thirled to the Church of Scotland, enlivened by Ignatian spirituality, I offer spiritual accompaniment and find new ploys even in my old age.

Karen Kinloch was born in 1969 with Down's syndrome and though now severely disabled with arthritis still manages to enjoy life, playing piano, keyboard and organ and, if there is an accessible pool, swims a mile twice weekly. She brings a lot of joy to her extended family and many friends, including those on the Internet.

S Anne Lawson is Vicar of the Cross Country Parishes of Acton, Church Minshull, Worleston and Wettenhall in South Cheshire. She shares her home with two rescue cats, Solomon and Shadow, who are, of course, in charge.

Susan Lindsay: 'I live in Fife with my chickens and kitten. I am a big fan of Monty Don.'

Jo Love is a Resource Worker with the Wild Goose Resource Group. Her passions include long solitary walks, playing with art and words, and conversations that reach places beyond your usual after-church coffee. Her dream dinner guest would be Ecclesiastes.

Rebeka Maples is Director of Spiritual Formation for the United Methodist Church programme Course of Study School of Ohio at Methodist Theological School in Ohio. She is retired from parish ministry, after serving churches in England and the U.S. She is an associate member of the Iona Community.

Peter Millar is a theologian, activist and writer who worked in India for many years. A former Warden of Iona Abbey, he has written widely on the relationship between the Christian faith and the hopes and struggles of our world today. For the last four years he has lived with an incurable cancer.

James Munro: 'I was born in a Fife mining village, and so Scots was my native language. After a working life spent teaching French at university level, I am now retired, and a member of Alva Parish Church, where from time to time I contribute pieces in Scots and English for the choir to sing.'

John Murning: 'I was born and bred in Airdrie, worked as an ice-cream salesman, Engineer and civil servant, before ministering in Cathcart, Bute, Denny and Paisley, with a diversion to Army Chaplaincy in Ripon and Kosovo. I am married to Linda and have two grown-up children.'

Katy Owen is a member of the Iona Community. She enjoys working in care homes and in the Lodging House Mission.

Avis Palmer is a Methodist Local Preacher in the North Cheshire Circuit and is a volunteer with Retreat House Chester, where she has led Quiet Days. She loves poetry, traditional and contemporary Gaelic songs and meditation music from Nepal and Tibet.

Sarah Pascoe: 'I'm an ex-nurse, mother and grandmother. I live beside the sea at the mouth of the Tyne.'

Jan Sutch Pickard is a poet, storyteller and preacher living in the Isle of Mull. She is a former Deputy Warden and Warden of Iona Abbey.

Chris Polhill is a gardener in both soil and soul.

Benjamin Pratt is a United Methodist minister who worked for many years as a pastoral counsellor. He is an advocate for caregivers and an author. His books include *A Guide for Caregivers* and *Short Stuff from the Tall Guy: Lenten Meditations on Seeking Peace in a Troubled World*. Benjamin lives near Washington DC with his wife, Judith.

Janet Pybon: 'I am a former Religious Studies teacher, currently serving as a Methodist minister in Lancashire, with a passion for promoting social justice and inclusion. My interests include reading, listening to music, creative writing and spending time appreciating the variety and beauty of creation – whether it is to be found in other people or in the natural world.'

John Rackley is a restless spirit who lives in Leicestershire.

John Randall: 'I've lived on the edge of Dartmoor for almost fifty years. I worked in social care and am now a licensed lay minister in our local cluster of churches.'

Julie Rennick is a Church of Scotland parish minister and regular contributor to Spill the Beans. She spends her leisure time exploring the Scottish landscape in a motor home with her husband and dogs.

Katherine Rennie is a member of the Iona Community and a Local Preacher with the Methodist Church. She is a retired solicitor and family mediator.

Margaret Roe is a retired Methodist Minister, living near Lincoln where she still has an active ministry, preaching and teaching. She has recently self-published two books: *Courage, Risk and Challenge: Women of the Old Testament Tell Their Stories* (Vols 1 and 2) and is currently working on a similar book about women mentioned in the Acts of the Apostles and Paul's letters.

The Rev'd Sr Sandra Sears, CSBC is a Local Priest in the Anglican Diocese of Willochra in rural South Australia, and a member of the Community of Sts Barnabas and Cecilia. As well as writing poetry, stories and liturgical resources, she is a composer of songs and hymns.

Richard Sharples is a Methodist minister currently living in Bristol, where he ministers to three churches which straddle the centre of the city. He loves to cycle, garden, walk and endeavours to weave some poetry into his life and prayers.

Robert Shooter: 'A teacher, seeing creative writing in my jotter as opposed to the formal English for his set work, said to me, "Why don't you write like that for me?" I have tried to ever since and, with the help of a Masters in Writing Studies from Edge Hill University, to enable others to find their voice.'

About the authors

Thom M Shuman is an associate member of the Iona Community and a frequent contributor to Wild Goose books. Though retired, he pastors a small church in Columbus, Ohio, and writes every day.

George Stuart is a thinker who is not willing to accept without question what he has been taught by the church. He has been an analytical Chemist, Clergyman, Personnel Manager and Rehabilitation Counsellor, but most importantly he is a husband, father and grandfather. He is 84 years young and looks forward to new challenges. He lives in beautiful Australia. He is always amazed about how wonderful humans can be.

Simon Taylor is a local Baptist minister and university chaplain in Exeter. For him, summer is a time for growing raspberries and sweet peas, and hoping for butterflies to visit his garden buddleia.

Bonnie Thurston resigned a Professorship in New Testament to live quietly in her home state of West Virginia. She gardens, is the author of many books, including *From Darkness to Eastering* (Wild Goose Publications, 2017), and volunteers at a food pantry.

Roberta van Biezen: In movement with All that surrounds us, in deep respect, in an all-encompassing Love and Gratitude for All.

Kit Walkham is a Methodist local preacher in Devon, who enjoys writing drama to get people thinking and has contributed a number of sketch scripts to www.theworshipcloud.com. She volunteers for Radius, the religious drama society, and ArtServe, a Christian arts network.

Rev. Mary Whittaker is Deaf and a Church of Scotland minister to Deaf people in North East Scotland and in the Highlands and Islands. She lives with a hearing dog called Scott and two cats.

Index of authors

A class of seven-year-olds 68
Angie Allport 230

Gill Bailey 212
Helen Barrett 39, 108
Stuart Barrie 19, 310
Elizabeth Baxter 187
Jan Berry 18, 200, 208, 256, 264, 270, 274, 275, 288, 318
Keith Blackwood 59
Ruth Bowen 290
Ruth Burgess 14, 24, 29, 37, 38, 44, 46, 47, 54, 56, 62, 64, 80, 81, 83, 92, 96, 101, 102, 136, 174, 201, 203, 232, 235, 252, 299, 305, 316
Scott Burton 84

Elizabeth Clark 72
Roddy Cowie 52, 61, 186, 192, 281, 311
Kathy Crawford 177
Liz Crumlish 298

da Noust 314
Liz Delafield 68, 155, 185, 193, 286
Judy Dinnen 78, 207, 265, 276, 284, 294
Carol Dixon 22, 153

Paul Fillery 124
Brian Ford 165, 196, 257
Alma Fritchley 269

Terry Garley 164
Tom Gordon 266
Louise Gough 30, 153, 175, 182, 279
Liz Gregory-Smith 19, 160, 214, 258

Becky Grisell 297

Roddy Hamilton 71, 98, 178
Mary Hanrahan 17, 158, 294
Pam Hathorn 151
J Mary Henderson 290
Brian Hick 168, 258
Jean Hudson 161, 163

Ian (aged 7) 265

Sally Howell Johnson 268
Peter Johnston 58

Janet Killeen 16, 48
Helen Kinloch 306
Karen Kinloch 267

S Anne Lawson 76, 182, 309
Susan Lindsay 249
Jo Love 89, 104, 107, 110, 113, 114, 116, 122, 123, 148, 180, 183, 226, 227, 238, 239

Rebeka Maples 130, 131, 132, 133, 134
Peter Millar 166
James Munro 43, 280
John Murning 70, 94, 125, 149, 172, 176, 194, 223, 228, 242

Katy Owen 73

Avis Palmer 152, 264, 271, 274
Sarah Pascoe 278
Jan Sutch Pickard 282
Chris Polhill 172, 191, 192
Benjamin Pratt 250, 296
Janet Pybon 244

John Rackley 74, 304
John Randall 16, 158, 260
Julie Rennick 125
Katherine Rennie 259
Margaret Roe 120

Sr Sandra Sears, CSBC 62, 220, 240
Richard Sharples 21, 279, 315
Robert Shooter 302
Thom M Shuman 231, 300
Spill the Beans 65, 96, 204, 238
George Stuart 28, 215

Simon Taylor 162, 200, 209, 218, 248, 253, 289, 314, 315, 317
Bonnie Thurston 20, 159, 163, 261

Roberta van Biezen 167, 308

Kit Walkham 86, 90, 210
Mary Whittaker 262, 291

Wild Goose Publications, the publishing house of the Iona Community established in the Celtic Christian tradition of Saint Columba, produces books, e-books, CDs and digital downloads on:

- holistic spirituality
- social justice
- political and peace issues
- healing
- innovative approaches to worship
- song in worship, including the work of the Wild Goose Resource Group
- material for meditation and reflection

For more information:

Wild Goose Publications
The Iona Community
21 Carlton Court, Glasgow, G5 9JP, UK

Tel. +44 (0)141 429 7281
e-mail: admin@ionabooks.com

or visit our website at
www.ionabooks.com
for details of all our products and online sales